from Hau
+ Dave

ACTIONS MIGHTIER THAN BOASTINGS

For Carol,
Church lady to
church lady!
Love, Dot.

Hope you
enjoy - Ann

ACTIONS MIGHTIER THAN BOASTINGS

Dr. Dot Radius Kasik
with Ann Aalgaard

back channel press
portsmouth, new hampshire

ACTIONS MIGHTIER THAN BOASTINGS
Copyright © 2009 by Dorothy Kasik
ISBN 13: 978-1-934582-15-2
ISBN 10: 1-934582-15-8

BACK CHANNEL PRESS
170 Mechanic Street
Portsmouth, NH 03801
www.backchannelpress.com
Printed in the United States of America

Design and layout by Nancy Grossman

Publisher's Cataloging-In-Publication Data
(Prepared by The Donohue Group, Inc.)

Kasik, Dot Radius.
  Actions mightier than boastings / Dot Radius Kasik, Ann Aalgaard.

    p. ; cm.

  Includes bibliographical references and index.
  ISBN-13: 978-1-934582-15-2
  ISBN-10: 1-934582-15-8

1. Women in church work--Iowa--Lutheran Church--20th century. 2. Women in church work--Minnesota--Lutheran Church--20th century. 3. Norwegian Americans--Iowa--20th century. 4. Norwegian Americans--Minnesota--20th century. 5. Women--Iowa--Societies and clubs--20th century. 6. Women--Minnesota--Societies and clubs--20th century. 7. Christian women--Religious life. 8. Evangelical Lutheran Church. 9. Women's Missionary Federation (Evangelical Lutheran Church) I. Aalgaard, Ann, 1966- II. Title.

BX8074.W65 K38 2009
284.1/31/082   2009922831

For

Elma, Clara, and Agnes

Acknowledgements

Without the Ladies of three very special Lutheran congregations, this book would not have been written. I am grateful for the time and enthusiasm that each of them has given me during this project. Many touched my life as I researched and wrote, but a few require special mention. Thank you to Ellen Bjelland, Viola Gavle, Berdine Honsey, and Pastor Julie Fisk at Emmons Lutheran Church; to Esther Thompson, Ruth Edwards, and Pastor Perry Aalgaard at Bethlehem Lutheran Church; to Vi and Einer Oppedahl, Hermoine Eilertson, Gwen Rowley, and Beverly Aalgaard at Trinity Lutheran Church. Between the beginnings of my research and the publishing of this book, Hermoine, Gwen, and Esther joined the "vast cloud of witnesses," a fact that reminds me to appreciate the others moment by moment.

Special thanks also goes to my long-time friend Addie Rolands; to Rev. (Ret.) Harvey Gilbertson and Esther Gilbertson; to Evelyn Stadheim and Jan Jerdee; and to the members of Holy Trinity Lutheran Church in Portsmouth, New Hampshire.

I am grateful for guidance and encouragement from the staff at Back Channel Press, and to Professor L. DeAne Lagerquist of St. Olaf College, Northfield, Minnesota.

Most especially, thanks goes to my sister and co-researcher, Ann Aalgaard, and to my husband, Kurt. Ann spent many hours in fact-checking, writing, editing, and advising. Through the entire process, Kurt has remained unfailingly patient and supportive.

Having so vast a cloud of witnesses surrounding us, let us lay aside every weight, and run with perseverance the race set before us. (Hebrews 12:1)

TABLE OF CONTENTS

INTRODUCTION
ACTIONS MIGHTIER THAN BOASTINGS

This is the story of the women in four small churches along the Iowa-Minnesota border, 1930-1959. The churches are Lutheran, and because of their locations, their membership is largely of Norwegian ancestry. My sister Ann and I embarked on this project because we were curious about the church lives of the women in our family. Our mother Agnes, our grandmother Clara, our aunts and great aunts were all pillars in the Ladies Aids of these congregations. Although already two and three generations away from Norwegian immigrant status, their ethnicity remained strong; bound up in that ethnicity was their Lutheran faith. From word of mouth, from stories we'd heard them tell, and from the example of their lives, we knew that their work and the work of their contemporaries was a primary reason that these four little congregations remained vibrant and useful.

We wanted to tell the story of these women, and that desire takes on urgency as we watch the generations passing. By the time we began, our grandmother's generation was already completely gone; we are now rapidly losing the next. And so we set about talking to the women to understand something about their church lives in the Ladies Aid, what roles the Ladies Aid played in maintaining day-to-day church activity, how the Ladies Aid connected these women to the broader church community, and how their work eventually affected our own faith lives. As we shared our intentions, we were struck by the women's certain knowledge that without the Ladies Aid of the 1930s, '40s, and '50s, today's Lutheran church would be much different.

These decades correspond to the active church lives of our mothers and grandmothers, but they also present as a period of particular growth for American Lutherans, more so in identity than in numbers. The '30s, '40s, and '50s encompass a time of increasing stability among Lutherans in the United States as the church Americanized itself. By 1930 several smaller synods had come together: the Norwegian Lutheran Church had become the United Lutheran Church, and the Iowa, Ohio, Texas, and Buffalo Synods had merged to become the American Lutheran Church. These mergers provided a 30-year interlude of synodical calm during which time local memberships could devote their energies to practical aspects such as raising monies for missions and ministering to their members. Not that the Lutheran church of these decades was ultimately finished organizing—future mega-mergers in 1960 and 1988 would produce first the American Lutheran Church (not the same as above) and then the present Evangelical Lutheran Church in America. However, arguably, the unified vision enjoyed by the ELCA today was shaped between 1930 and 1959.

Outside of the church, the years before, during, and immediately after World War II were a time when America was occupied with redefining itself from a simple, somewhat motley collection of immigrants to world superpower. As a nation, we worked to understand our emerging position in relation to other nations. Isolationism hadn't worked, but during world conflict, a wave of nationalism brought strength and unity. As the nation worked to form a cohesive identity over and above individual ethnicities, so too Lutherans increasingly saw themselves as part of a greater whole.

In the upper Midwest, Norwegian Americans redefined themselves to the wider population. In a nation eager to demonstrate thorough Americanism both to the world and itself, ethic peoples formerly identified with an individual ethnicity as their defining adjective began to fit themselves into the wider population; *Norwegian* Americans suddenly saw themselves as Americans of Norwegian ancestry, or *American* Norwegians. The change affected all areas of life, whether social, political, educational, or religious. One obvious way Americanization manifested itself in Lutheran churches was the switch in language. Parishes that had been slow to upgrade now traded in Norwegian services for English. Efforts in Americanization were almost militant and would span three decades in the immigrant Norwegian community, throughout an entire generation's coming of age. By mid-century the transformation would be complete. In *Norwegians in Minnesota*, Jon Gjerde and Carlton C. Qualey write that by 1950, "the Norwegian America of [an earlier age] was no longer visible…" (70). We now take Americanism for granted.

Our purpose here is not to record the complete history of Lutherans or the Lutheran Church for the period; we present only a quick overview of what the women themselves have helped us to see as the basis for what defines both them and the age. It is our hope that readers might avail themselves of some of the fine histories that have been and are being written about these decades, some of which are listed in our bibliography.

Five decades have intervened since 1959. In the Midwestern Norwegian community, dispersed and assimilated as it is, few remember the immigrant experience. Stored away in our attics, the trunks of our ancestors bear late 19th-century dates. If we're lucky enough to have them, those first precious letters from parents, siblings or lovers left behind in the Old Country are pressed between the pages of old Bibles. Today, Norwegian identity is something we take out and try on for festival occasions. We might spend family vacations visiting the places left behind, tramping through graveyards in Voss and Bergen and Trondheim, and return home with Christmas sweaters, troll figurines, and a national costume to wear in the local Leif Erikson parade. We might even take a few Norwegian language classes. But our generation's desire for ethnicity is of a completely new form than our ancestor's identity with it. In the words of Jon Gjerde and Carlton C. Qualey in *Norwegians in Minnesota*, ours is "symbolic" ethnicity.

In the past, Norwegians lived their Norwegian folkways, speaking Norwegian on the street and in their churches. Present "symbolic" ethnicity is different from an ethnic allegiance based on an immigrant past. The interest of many Norwegian Americans in their ancestral culture is more casual. They are Americans curious about their backgrounds, not Norwegian immigrants trying to become Americans (70, 71).

My sister and I are curious about our ethnicity. We're equally curious about how Lutheranism flourished through it, curious about how our family remained Lutheran, and curious about the intersections between Norwegian ethnicity and Lutheranism. Listening to the Ladies Aid women still living, we begin to understand how and why we're able to take our Lutheran identity for granted. We get a glimpse of the Lutheran calm between 1930 and 1959—again, induced through twin drives toward unification and Americanization—which paved the way for our identity, and we're hungry to learn more. Happily, all the Aid members we interviewed, women who themselves understand both the gains and losses incurred in assimilating a culture, were more than willing to feed our hunger. We hope that examining their church lives will teach us how the Lutheran Ladies Aid connects us to our past, perhaps in turn connecting us to our future.

METHODS

A few words about our research methodology are necessary.

The number and identity of the congregations we chose to include in our study developed in a practical way. From the inception of our project, we knew we wanted to focus on women's testimonies. Originally we'd intended to cut a rather wide swathe, taking in most or all of the churches along the central Minnesota-Iowa border, churches in a region that had been populated mostly by Scandinavians during the latter years of the

1800's. Norwegian Lutheran was our family experience, so it was natural to make those congregations our field of study. Early in our project, we realized the number had to be contained, so we narrowed our focus to four of what we regarded as our "home" churches. First is Emmons Lutheran in Emmons, Minnesota, where we spent our childhoods and where women held their first Ladies Aid meeting in 1896, six years before the church itself was established. In 1960 Emmons built the facility where they currently worship, but prior to that, the congregation was housed in a typical small, white clapboard building close to the center of town. It boasted a white steeple, a tin-ceilinged sanctuary, and the ubiquitous basement where all the social life of the congregation was carried out.

In those days Emmons was a two-point congregation, sharing ministerial support with Lime Creek Lutheran, where our mother had belonged as a child. Organized in 1874, Lime Creek was three miles away and similar to Emmons Lutheran in architecture. Their first official Ladies Aid event is recorded as a "hand-made goods sale" in 1885. Because of the family connections, it felt natural to make Lime Creek our second choice, even though it no longer exists—the formal congregation has been disbanded and the building moved to the grounds of a living-history museum.

Our third church is Trinity Lutheran in Bricelyn, Minnesota. Founded in 1879 with the Ladies Aid following in 1887, Trinity is the childhood church of Ann's husband Perry and a church they and their children attended together for several years. Our fourth congregation is Bethlehem Lutheran in Buffalo Center, Iowa, where Perry presently serves as pastor. Bethlehem's Ladies Aid was organized in 1893.

Having limited ourselves to four congregations, we set about arranging interviews with senior members from each, women who had been active for many years in one of the congregations (or in a few cases, holding consecutive memberships in two of the four). The women range in age from mid-70s to 98, which means their experience as Ladies Aid members dates from the early 1930s. Some of them are women we knew as we grew up. Some were recommended to us by church secretaries and pastors.

When possible, interviews were conducted in the subjects' homes. With permission, we taped each conversation. For some of the interviews, a husband was present and was invited to contribute to the discussion. Sometimes our subjects had photographs or keepsake documents such as invitations, programs, and bulletins from special events to share with us. The interviews, more than anything else, provided material for the stories we tell.

In addition to interviews, we collected and examined written documents from three of the four congregations (excepting Lime Creek). Local church historians over the years kept minutes of meetings, copies of constitutions and by-laws, and financial records. Annual reports were invaluable. In addition, historians collected bulletins and programs from special events and celebrations, newspaper articles, invitations to events, and program scripts. The three active congregations recently celebrated their centennials; in preparation, materials had been carefully collected and sorted—circumstances whose benefits we reaped.

There were times when we were led to a series of broader investigations, times when the documents or the women themselves opened questions that needed answers or created rabbit trails that needed following. These led us to various experts on church history, museums and libraries—like the Luther Resource Center in Clear Lake, Iowa, and the libraries at the St. Paul Seminary—and the internet, including the ELCA Archives.

As we reviewed our transcripts and began writing, it became increasingly obvious to us that there were pieces of information that couldn't be easily attributed. There were ideas presented to us in group discussions, for instance, about which we'd made notes but for which we couldn't name specific sources. There were conversations that occurred spontaneously when we had neither note paper nor tape recorder but from which we learned important facts. There were feelings. To solve the problem of shaping and recording such information, we invented "characters" to aid us; gradually, eventually, as time went on, the characters became live. We are the first to admit that such inventions flirt with what could be considered spurious methodology. Nevertheless, the vehicle first devised to fill in our spaces turned itself into three distinct and strong personalities. Alma, Marita, and Linnea were born.

Alma, Marita, and Linnea are fictional characters on an historical stage. More than figments of imagination, they are collective presences. As we researched, these three helped us think through and put into context conversations with real people, some of whom didn't want their names used, others whose conversations echoed in our minds but didn't appear on tapes or notes. In the process of collection and reflection, we talked to Alma, Marita, and Linnea as much as listened to them, especially during many of those times when we needed to reach back beyond our own memories to "feel" or experience whatever the Ladies were telling us. They accompanied Ann and me to interviews (where they were mostly courteously silent). They were with us as we searched through historical documents, photo albums, old meeting minutes, and financial ledgers. They looked over our shoulders at libraries and museums. Once back home we summoned them to help us make sense of everything we'd read or heard. They were unfailingly patient. They pointed out gaps and inconsistencies in our thinking. When they didn't know the answers, they urged us back to talk again with one of the Ladies.

BACKGROUND

Alma, Marita, and Linnea are second and third generation Americans, living in small towns and nearby farms between 1930 and 1959, sometimes having access to a family automobile, sometimes not. Along the state line between Minnesota and Iowa, they were still mostly of Norwegian or other northern European ancestry and mostly descendants of Lutherans. Their ancestors were people schooled in Pontoppidan Lutheranism by a state church. Under the conflation of government and church, civic experience was a prescribed life. Coming to the New World where church and government were independent of each other stripped them of such prescription. In America church leadership was neither appointed nor supported by government. Church policy did not equal public policy.

At least the first generation, and in some places the second as well, had a shortage of ordained leadership. The first Norway clergy didn't arrive until late in the nineteenth century. Norwegian Americans knew they'd have to find a way to produce their own religious leaders, and so Lutheran colleges were founded in the main to train men for the ministry—i.e., Luther College in Decorah, Iowa, in 1861, and St. Olaf College in Northfield, Minnesota, in 1874. But the day-to-day, week-by-week, practice of faith was handled much more individually. How it happened in those days that Lutheranism hung together as a unified body of doctrine at all is a question that fuels our interest in women's church leadership. The women we write about are a product of people who must have held the articles of their faith very deeply for it to have survived on the Great Plains into the twentieth century more or less intact from the European experience.

Whether second, third, or even fourth generation Americans, the women in this project are a transitional generation. It was during their lifetimes that the family car evolved from oddity to norm and women drivers from rarity to given. Most of them—at least the rural women—began their lives without indoor plumbing. Some remember when the Rural Electric Cooperative arrived. Many attended one-room school houses. Their childhoods were lived without television but (if they were lucky) with party-line phone service. Now in their 70s, 80s, and 90s, they play DVDs on their televisions, chat with their grandchildren over e-mail, and carry cell phones whenever they leave the house. They've lived through momentous historical events: the Stock Market Crash and Great

Depression, WWII, Korea, Viet Nam, the fall of the USSR, the creation of the European Common Market, space flight, the eradication of polio and the emergence of HIV/AIDs, open heart surgery and organ transplants, the discovery of DNA and genetic engineering, and an inter-connected electronic world that brings every event into their living rooms simultaneous to its happening. Amazing.

Above all, our women are women of *service*. In the words of one of our interviewees, 84-year-old Vi, a former Aid officer, "The Ladies Aid was always all about doing for others. We *served*." It is in this idea—in their self-identified vocation of service—that we find our title. The introduction to a discussion of Ladies Aid work in the *75th Anniversary Book of the Emmons Lutheran Church*, written in 1979, reads, "These women went about their Ladies Aid work in an unassuming and unpretentious way, and there were no records kept of meetings except perhaps a report of money taken in or given away. To them it seemed, 'Deeds are better things than words, and *actions mightier than boastings.*'" No, they didn't boast. They served. Unlike the first generations of immigrants whose energies were occupied in establishing church communities, by 1930 the Lutheran Church was firmly enough entrenched on the Plains that women were free to turn their attention to quietly doing for others.

Because the Ladies' focus was always on doing service rather than writing about it, much of their story has never been told. Their importance to, their contributions toward, and their shaping of the present Lutheran church has not been talked about enough. They were "basement women," noted by the name of a popular cookbook, and that in itself reveals why much of their story is untold: their physical work was more often than not accomplished in church basements. Financially, spiritually, and socially their work was the foundation of all other church work, but it was often disregarded and belittled, hidden away, kept off official church records and ignored at district, convention, and synod levels. As L. DeAne Lagerquist writes in *In America the Men Milk the Cows*, because women's stated purpose was to *support* the work of the church, they were excluded from leadership. Yet by no means were they non-influential. Ladies Aid groups provided women with a "channel of local influence," through which their financial contributions gave them a say in virtually every decision (148).

Talk to today's Women of the Evangelical Lutheran Church of America (WELCA) members who are in their 70s, 80s, and 90s about their church work and like as not you'll hear them lapse into calling themselves the "Aid," but the Lutheran church by no means had a lock on the term. Ladies Aid societies have been and still are present in denominations from Roman Catholic to Presbyterian to Baptist. The term was also applied to women's civic and social organizations outside the church. It flourished nationally in the years surrounding the Civil War when women's organizations formed at an unprecedented rate, supporting religious, social, and political causes ranging from medical support of injured Civil War soldiers to birth control, temperance, and women's suffrage. Where the term originated we don't know, but in Norwegian Lutheran churches in the Midwest, it replaced *kvindeforeninger* (women's societies) as English replaced the Norwegian language in a congregation. Here it named adult women's support groups. It was the name used both locally and district or conference-wide for church women's organizations, even though they were separate units of the larger Women's Missionary Federation. Then in 1960, when four separate synods merged to form the American Lutheran Church, the women's organization of the new body was given a new name, new organizational structure, and newly elected leadership at the district level and above. Things changed even at the local level as individual congregations welcomed synodical support in the forms of leadership and literature afforded by the new organization. Nevertheless, the women we interviewed lapsed into calling themselves Aid members as they talked about their local groups. The name still says something to them about how they view themselves and how they view the service they render to their church. In truth, many women hardly missed a beat as they were reorganized and directed into being the ALCW, then a few years later into

WELCA. Indeed, on the local level, the structural organization of the groups remains very much the same.

Ladies Aids were support groups. Their mission was to assist the local congregation in day-to-day responsibilities, including care of membership, hosting of congregational events, general maintenance of the physical facility, and continued religious training of members. They also took on the responsibility of missions, providing charitable support for the surrounding community and overseas concerns. Ladies Aid was definitely "other"-centered. It was also self-centered, but in the very healthiest definition of that term. While the women aided others, they aided themselves. The women might have invested most of their practical energies maintaining home congregations and earning money for charities, but the arguably greater mission was that members provided emotional and spiritual support for each other. The Ladies Aid was the center of life.

The Lutheran Ladies Aid as it operated through the Women's Missionary Federation is largely gone, but it will not be our intent in this project to center on lost aspects of the Aid, although certainly there are losses when the mission and membership of any organization changes. One of the first things we noticed when we met with members or attended today's meetings is a change in demographics. Churches that boasted 150 women in attendance at monthly meetings in the '50s feel fortunate today when 20 members show up. The median age of attendees has risen from mid-40s to mid-70s. Some of the activities and some of the styles of support practiced in the '30s, '40s, and '50s have been outgrown. As women in the second half of the twentieth century entered the professional work force in increasing numbers, typical patterns of daytime meetings and service became impractical. The ordination of women as pastors in the '70s opened new conversations about gender roles and leadership requirements. American life has changed. Needs have changed. As times change, the church moves on to meet them.

But as we move on, we need to recognize the work of people who paved the way for us to make the kinds of social changes we now embrace. Women of the old Aid who still remember and can tell us what it was like are getting older. We won't have them with us much longer. Their stories are wonderful: inspiring, delightful, funny, and—most of all—educational. Our project is to begin to tell some of them and hopefully to encourage others to do the same. We want this to be a way to honor the women who exemplified the role of service and encouraged the development of faith; women who through selfless work, frustration, tears, and joy evolved the Lutheran church into what it is for us today. We cannot forget. We owe much to the Ladies of the Women's Missionary Federation.

CHAPTER ONE
I LOVE TO TELL THE STORY

Deeds are better things than words, and actions mightier than boastings.
-75th Anniversary Book of the Emmons Lutheran Church
as quoted from Henry Wadsworth Longfellow's "Hiawatha"

"Call us Ladies!" She said it with a wink and a smile and a slight shift of her 86-year-old hips. Alma of course was drawing on the image of the white gloves, hat, and prim little shirtwaist she'd worn for Ladies Aid meetings in the '50s. And she said it to emphasize the change in costume—today she sported denim jeans and her hot pink sweatshirt emblazoned across the chest with "Iowa You Make Me Smile!"—as well as the change in attitude of the Ladies themselves.

Sixty-five years ago when Alma joined the Ladies Aid she had a whole collection of cute little hats to wear to meetings. "It could sometimes be a bit of a fashion show. Generally speaking, Aid meetings and church were the two places we had for real dress-up. Only problem was with 150 of us all dressed up and all buying from The Merchantile downtown, you'd likely see yourself coming and going when you looked around!"

"But we did dress for the meetings. It just showed how important it was."

My sister Ann and I talk with Alma in a meeting room at Emmons Lutheran. This is Alma's home church. At the far end our space is appointed with a sofa and occasional chairs pulled into a conversation area.

Opposite is a mini kitchen—the kind you might find in a hotel suite, except that the table seats eight. A third wall is lined with windows, the fourth with floor-to-ceiling shelves where the spines of Bibles and fat brown commentaries alternate with children's picture books, crisp inspirational titles on marriage and childrearing, and, of course, well-worn Christian novels.

After the first few minutes, Alma's friends Marita from Trinity Lutheran and Linnea from Bethlehem Lutheran join us. They've come to teach us about Ladies Aid. On average, three women like Alma, Marita, and Linnea collectively hold 175 to 200 years of Ladies Aid membership, depending on whether their enrollments date from the 1930s or 1940s or 1950s. That's a lot of combined Aid knowledge. They have much to teach us.

"Alma," "Marita," and "Linnea" are our mothers, our sisters, our aunts, and our grandmothers. They are teachers, friends, and mentors. Their children and grandchildren went to school with us. We played after-school games in their back yards. Today they listen to our questions with bemusement. We've told them that we want to write about them, about the Lutheran Ladies Aid of the 1930s, '40s, and '50s. Ladies Aid is something they love and value. It has always been and remains a center for their social and spiritual lives. Whether the conversation is about their own life in Ladies Aid or in the life of their congregation, they don't have to be convinced of its importance. However, when it comes to each woman talking about her *personal* contributions to history, no one finds it easy. There's a reticence in talking about themselves. We see them as protagonists in a continuing story, and that makes them a little uncomfortable. They take what they've done pretty much for granted. The way they see it, there was work to be done, and they were the ones to do it. If the result is that Lutheran faith, life, and values have been both shaped and preserved, well, that's a good thing, but no need to crow about it!

Today we meet "Alma," "Marita," and "Linnea" in the library. On another day it'll be Ida, Thelma, Kathryn, and Mavis in fellowship hall. Or

Esther and Shirley at the retirement home. Gertrude in her kitchen. Geri and Louise at a local coffee shop. Adeline at the park. Some of the women remember us as children of the congregation. A few taught us in Sunday school. Many knew our mother, our aunts, our grandmother. When we explain our project—to write about how the Lutheran Ladies Aid of their generation shaped a faith experience for our generation—they're eager to contribute and patient with our questions...but bemused.

If Alma, Marita, and Linnea were patient, they were also expert. We found them all throughout the historical literature, whether we were reading from local Ladies Aid historical files, from newspaper accounts of one of our churches, or from history written by professionals. Much of the history of churches was recorded throughout the ages by women, and many times they remained as invisible as these three. Church secretaries, even council secretaries, were often women, even in the early days. Without the ability to vote or even speak publicly, they were crafting memories for us. Ann and I began to consciously think of them as our invisible historians when we named them Alma, Marita, and Linnea. Lutheran historian and theologian L. DeAne Lagerquist writes in *In America the Men Milk the Cows* that "Religious historians have provided women with very few opportunities to speak about their vigorous participation in the church's life. Congregational historians, some of them women, have been more attentive to the role women have played" (4).

As we "listen" to them we learn that Alma, now 86, married and entered the Ladies Aid in 1942. At 95, Marita is the oldest. She was first elected to Aid office in 1935. Linnea, 84, served during the '50s as a district delegate from Bethlehem.

Alma takes for granted we understand what she's talking about when she talks about Aid. She doesn't begin at the beginning of the story but plunges in at the middle. "We had us some good times, we did. I remember a lot about the meals and such, cooking, serving; and Marita here can talk about the Circles. How they were organized. She's the quilter. And then

Linnea was District officer who went to all those area meetings. But we were all together way back when it was just 'Aid' and we're still together now when it's WELCA. Still running things, we are!"

We laugh in agreement. We've been to one of the WELCA meetings, and we know they're right. However, Ann's and my field of interest right now is long before WELCA and even before ALCW, back to the days after the giant Lutheran merger of 1930 to form the church body that would support Women's Missionary Federation (WMF), which in turn supported the Ladies Aids of Emmons, Bethlehem, Trinity, and Lime Creek Lutheran Churches. These three women—and the others of their age group who were active in the WMF—remember these years as somewhat golden. As we listened, we thought we could hear at least three overarching themes emerge as climatic reasons for why the decades between 1930 and 1960 produced golden years for the Ladies Aid. The first is that by this time in history, the members were second and third generation Americans, secure in an American Lutheran identity. In a parallel manner, the Lutheran Ladies Aid too was into its third generation, which meant that most organizational issues that might have presented difficulty for their mothers or grandmothers had been thoroughly thought through. The WMF provided structure, support, instruction, and direction but wasn't so commanding as to prevent individuality among local chapters. Secondly, a series of national crises—notably the Depression, World War II, and Korea—encouraged women within church groups to band together under the desire to do something to solve conditions around them. They looked to the WMF to give them venues for action. Thirdly, while industry and technology were beginning to make life easier and more accessible through such innovations as family vehicles, telephones, radio, and finally television, those things were still new enough that they hadn't completely changed the fabric of social life in the States. Here in rural America, most families had an automobile by then (a family car—or if was a farming household—a pick up), but the "two car garage" wasn't yet in vogue. Most homes also had a telephone—just one, no extensions—on a party line they shared with a half dozen other families. The Rural Electric Association arrived in 1935, and nearly everyone had a radio. Still, compared with today, life was technologically simpler, and women looked to an organization like Aid to provide the bulk of social life.

"I don't think women today, especially the younger ones and if they don't have mothers or grandmothers who were Aid, know how important it was. Today they have jobs even if they have kids at home. And there are so many other things to do with their time."

"Oh, sure. I know like with my daughter, she's a stay-at-home mom (isn't it funny that there's a name for it now? We were just "moms") but she has so many activities with kids. She drives them to sports and after school activities and even play dates. Then she can't leave them alone these days—like my kids spent time on their own at home without me because you could do that then, but you can't now."

"Well, and organizations today can take so much of a person's time and interest. I'm not blaming anyone—I run to a lot of different kinds of meetings too: quilt club, book study, the library guild, committee this, committee that. But when we started in Ladies Aid, all of that was just part of it. We went to church for all of it."

"Or the senior center. The church was the senior center then. Sure. Like my grandma and that age group, they came to Aid even after they were too old to work, and everyone understood and helped them out. I remember one old lady whose daughter would bring her to every meeting and she sat with her knitting. She was almost blind, but there she sat with her knitting, and it meant she didn't have to be home alone."

"Well, and we did have to work hard. There wasn't a modern commercial kitchen like we have now."

"Oh, no, there sure wasn't. Remember how long it took us in the morning to get the heat up, get the water boiling for coffee?"

"Talking about boiling the water for coffee reminds me of one time when we were going to have a chicken dinner back in the days when the men would come at noontime and have their meal before going back to work. So this day we were scurrying around and getting everything ready, got the tables set and the chairs around, and then we realized no one had made the coffee! No coffee! You couldn't feed men without coffee!"

"No cleaning service, no hired babysitters, not even so much as laundry service for pastors' robes. Remember Pastor S, and how white he always wanted his robes? Oh, he was a picky one! He knew what he wanted."

"Well, but then he wasn't so bad as some you heard about. There were pastors who really expected that you'd be at the beck and call all the time, that the Aid existed as their personal servants. We were lucky that way. Not like my cousin Jane's church when their pastor called her up one day and asked—no, *ordered*—her to her to come and clean out his office. She had to order his books by alphabet for him!"

"Well, I know what I'd say to his request now. I'd tell him what he could do with his books!" This last brought on a fit of laughter until the Ladies were all wiping their eyes.

"We worked hard, but you know, I think it was better that way. There was never much money, it seemed; even after the Depression eased and the economy got straightened out. You didn't spend money on anything you could do yourself. You appreciated the value of things. And I think it made for more fun."

"You're right. We worked hard, but we worked together. Funny how you could hate having to cook a big meal at home but then come to church and do the same thing and have it be so fun."

We listen and laugh, and sometimes when I catch Ann's eye, we nod at each other in recognition. Some of the stories are legend enough that we've heard them before, from our grandmother, our aunts, and our mother. When Mom was still alive, we sisters used to look at each other and roll our eyes whenever she got started. We heard many of her stories dozens of times. We could recite some of them along with her. At the same time, we appreciated them and have grown to do so even more now and to understand some of the complicated purposes in her story-telling. Her stories were about people, about their strengths and weaknesses, their wisdom or shortsightedness, their triumphs and failures. They were never cruel or belittling, but often they were funny. Above all, every story had a purpose. Mom told stories about the people she knew because it was the best proof about what people are really like. Why was Margie C. the kindest woman she'd ever met? Insert story about Margie's being rescued from poverty. What made Jane W. such a good nurse? Insert story about her sister's gruesome struggle with cancer. How did Eugenia decide to become a high school teacher, then a college professor? Insert story about being tapped by her fifth grade teacher to set up a tutoring center in the cloakroom to work with younger students.

I've been writing as fast as I can, and I still haven't been able to keep up. Ann hasn't even made a pretense of note-taking; she was simply enjoying herself. I lay down my pen too.

"Oh, my! The memories just come flooding back now that we're talking!" Linnea sighs.

"I haven't thought of these things in years," adds Marita.

"See here what we've brought you!" Alma opens the tote bag I'd thought was simply a large purse and dumps the contents onto the table. Out spills an array. There are old yearbooks, service bulletins, certificates of recognition, black-and-white group photos, newspaper articles, and more. Several spiral-bound notebooks fall out. A couple of tiny spiral tablets, the sort Mom used to carry in her purse, are tangled together. At the bottom are two ancient ledgers. "I went through some boxes by the file cabinets and pulled stuff you might be interested in. We dug through lots of this for the 150-year celebration last year. The committee used it to do the historical write-up and got it all organized." Ann and I exchange amused glances. So much for organization.

The conversation turns now to specific memories as article after article is picked up and read aloud. Photos are shown around, and women either very elderly or long dead are pointed out.

"You see the hats and gloves?" Alma asks. I examine the picture she holds out.

"Here's our grandma," I point. "I actually remember that hat! What's the date on this one? Sometime in the '50s?"

Marita plucks the photo from my hand. "Yes, I'd say '55 or '56. Your grandma Clara was a fine lady."

And so the afternoon goes. Ann and I come away feeling slightly disoriented. We've spent the last hours living 50, 60, and 70 years in the past, beginning with recovery from World War I, isolationism and the switch from immigrant thinking to Americanism, through the Great Depression and World War II, and on to the Korean War before finally coming to 1959, the huge synodical merger into the American Lutheran Church, and the closing of the Women's Missionary Federation. It's time to part. We share hugs all around and make promises to meet next week. Alma, Marita, and Linnea leave for home and their individual supper preparations. Ann and I gather our notes, tapes, tape recorder, and camera.

THE BOX

The next Sunday afternoon we sisters sit at the old dining room table. We feel expectation, excitement, and even a little apprehension. We are about to open The Box.

Earlier in the week, Ann had talked with Esther and Ruth, lifelong members of Bethlehem Lutheran. They are close friends. They are women who love Bethlehem Lutheran and love history; they saw this as a chance to share those feelings with a wider audience. Nothing pleased them more than a chance to tell a good story. Ann heard about annual craft fairs, making quilts for Lutheran World Relief, driving to the city for a yearly synod convention, and arguing over how to assign unpleasant chores like janitorial work on an equitable basis. Esther and Ruth were treasure troves of facts. Before parting, they'd entrusted Ann with The Box.

The Box is where historical records from Bethlehem Lutheran Ladies Aid are kept. It is stored in a church closet under the responsibility of the last Ladies Aid historian (Ruth) before the Aid disbanded to become WELCA. It contains minutes and memorabilia dating back to the early 1930s. About the size of a U-Haul book box, it's hand fashioned from sheets of aluminum, folded and riveted together to make a (mostly) rectangular receptacle with fitted lid. We love The Box. We love the thought of The Box. It hides a story in and of itself. Whose husband fashioned it? Did he volunteer for the job? We like to imagine that he built it because he valued the women's history as much as they did.

And now we sit in front of Ruth's box. As with their stories, The Box has been entrusted to us in full faith that we'll treat it with respect and lose or harm nothing. More importantly, they trust that we'll see the importance, catch the excitement, and make known the stories to a wider audience. Making their stories part of the history of the church will be a validation of their work and faith. They know the stories themselves are *real* history, valued over and above official documents, synod decisions, records of district conventions, or anything else that gets cataloged by historians in seminary libraries. In their estimation, the history of Bethlehem Lutheran Ladies Aid is the history of the faith preserved in personal stories. How absolutely appropriate that the stories be housed in a homemade aluminum box!

What's in The Box? We lift the silvery lid. It doesn't come easily— neither lid nor box is truly square—so we have to wrangle it a bit. As it finally scrapes away, library mold wafts out. Its contents have lain dormant some time. We set about unpacking, making piles. On top is the organizational constitution for Bethlehem Ladies Aid and its by-laws; next come monthly Ladies Aid meeting minutes, annual Ladies Aid reports, year-by-year lists of elected officers, transcripts of programs and presentations, church bulletins, annual financial records, photographs, and lists of circle assignments. We lay things out across the table, keeping a chronological order as best we can, always mindful that aged documents are brittle. We know that these fragile papers hold the collective story of the women of Bethlehem Lutheran, told through incremental notations: dues collected, monies earned, projects funded. Records of achievement: certificates of merit, birthdays and anniversaries, graduations. Congregational landmarks: calling pastors, building campaigns, new member rosters. Passages of time: babies baptized, funerals served.

And more: the occasional odd note, as in "1934: $5 collected from Mrs. A. Anderson in lieu of serving." As we sift through, it's hard to refrain from imagining individual stories. Why didn't Mrs. Anderson serve? Was she widowed? Indigent? Ill? Was the arrangement her idea or someone else's? Maybe she was a poor cook, or ill, or a feminist before her time. Here among the piles as we read the cryptic entry, a dozen ill-fated food stories we've heard from interviews leap to memory: blind Selma's cupcakes are surreptitiously repaired, Alma's spoiled meat donation is quietly replaced, old Idy's flavorless casserole is hidden….but we're getting ahead of ourselves. Food stories need to wait for their appropriate chapter, and we need to keep to the business of sorting artifacts. It's easy to be diverted. Story is tantalizing. Each artifact, each notation, each scrap of recorded fact—how or why it was preserved—is a story nugget, needing only a gentle nudge to release a trove of meaning. Ruth knew all of that when she handed over The Box.

What's in this box is an attempt by women to tell future generations (us) how they spent their time and shaped their faith, all while keeping their church running. It tells us what they thought was important. It's an attempt at illustrating, preserving, testing, and validating their lives. It's an attempt to contain the life of a congregation of women.

We rummage. We notice physical details. The earliest documents are handwritten, mostly on lined ledger-style paper, some on plain white. Some pages have been torn from notebooks. Again, wisps of story tantalize. Individual handwriting can be recognized. ("Shea's" is particularly graceful, and we imagine her being chosen as recorder because of her penmanship.) The ink is mostly black, faded to sepia, scratched from fountain pen nibs that leave occasional characteristic blobs. (On one page is a blur around an attempt to correct a mistake, and I have a sudden picture of my own grandmother seated at her writing desk with a Q-tip, dabbing bleach on a misspelling.) One notable recorder has used green. (A nonconformist? An artist? Who would own a bottle of green ink?) Through the late '40s we begin to see typewritten materials; by mid-'50s all typewritten (Can you still buy onion skin?), some mimeographed. A sheaf of the earliest pages is fastened together with a straight sewing pin. As we dig through the years, a few paper clips appear, then finally staples.

We see that individual historians have distinct writing styles. The Box contains a yearly summary of Ladies Aid activities from 1930 through the '50s. We read the summaries, and we can tell without seeing the signature when the historical pen is passed. One historian is perfunctory about what she includes and how she says it. The next is more fluid, including little hints about individual personalities and comments about how events are received. We wonder aloud about how each of these women might have seen her role as historian. As she picked and chose what to include and how to format her account, no doubt each was conscious of how she herself might be read by a future generation.

Here in the silver box from Bethlehem Lutheran in Buffalo Center we see the efforts of women who knew it would be important for their daughters and granddaughters to know about the things that were so important to them. At Emmons Lutheran and Trinity Lutheran in Bricelyn, the Boxes are cardboard, but they too deliver fascinating, instructive glimpses into the lives of their respective Ladies Aids. Now one, two, and even three generations later, we "read" the Boxes. We read with gratitude and appreciation, with interest and with awe.

We also read with the same questions that shape our interviews. No matter how rich their contents, the collected artifacts can't really tell us the *story*. An annual report or an anniversary history tells us how much money was given to missions each year or how many people contributed to the building fund, but we have to talk to a live person to hear the discussions that decided which missions would be targeted or how a handful of women convinced their husbands that building fund money needed to be spent on a new kitchen. For that we need to turn to women who remember. The history of the Ladies Aid is kept in their memories. They have it catalogued in their stories. They're willing to share; we need to listen.

CHAPTER TWO
IN OUR HOMES AND UNDER THE TREES

At the turn of the twentieth century, many men considered the formation of church women's societies a new, radical, and even dangerous idea. When such organizations did manage to form, the congregation's pastor usually attended the meetings and led the program. After all, worried one alarmed pastor, if women were left to their own devices, "Who knows what they will pray for?"

-Susan Wilds McArver

FIRST PARISHES

In order to understand more about the women of the Evangelical Lutheran Church Ladies Aid or the Women's Missionary Federation, Alma, Marita, and Linnea take us back in time to learn something of their history. Ann and I research. We visit various Lutheran libraries and historical centers—like the Luther Resource Center in Clear Lake, Iowa, and the archival library at Luther Seminary in St. Paul, Minnesota—we plow through the Boxes, we dig through file cabinets, and we call on women who remember hearing their moms, aunts, and grandmas talk about earlier days of the Ladies Aids.

Gwen and Vi are members of Trinity Lutheran. Gwen has wild, white hair escaping from the bun at the back of her head. It flies out around her face and bobs with her head as she talks. "That picture over there is my mother. She was Sunday school superintendent and Aid president the same year. She was old, oh, she was almost 102. I mean, she wasn't president at 102. Oh, no, much younger." She chuckles at herself. "Mother was one of those who did a good share of the church history for the 100th anniversary celebration. I typed it for her. My grandmother before her was one of those who organized the Ladies Aid."

Vi is so tiny she has to stand on tiptoe to view her son's picture on her bookshelf. Diminutive but with boundless energy, Vi, like Gwen, comes from familial Ladies Aid tradition. "I lived in church all my life. I started going with my mom. I lived with my grandparents for a while, and my grandmother was one of those who was pretty active in the beginnings. I knew that Aid, going to Aid was important. I was pretty young, but I remember. Isn't that something?"

Although neither woman remembers the actual organization of their Ladies Aid, they were both close to the women who set things in motion. Their earliest memories include stories of how Trinity Ladies Aid began. In both cases, their own grandmothers helped in the organization. Now, more than a century removed from those earliest days, Ann and I depend on written histories—one typed by Gwen herself—and memories to piece together the story. Alma, Marita, and Linnea hover quietly nearby, helpful, thoughtful, whispering.

Much had to happen before the Ladies Aid of the '30s could come into being. A sizable population of Lutherans had to amass in the area. The national, political, and economic climates had to be inviting enough for local church bodies to form from which women's organizations could emerge. By the last decades of the nineteenth century, those conditions had been met, and for a Lutheran women's movement not to have appeared then would have been impossible. Ladies Aid was inevitable.

As early as 1853, under the leadership of Rev. C.L. Clausen, Silver Lake Synod had organized, encompassing the areas above—plus a few hundred additional square miles. By 1859, the Norwegian Evangelical Lutheran

Congregation of Silver Lake was solidified, and ten years later they called their first pastor. It was a lot of territory for one man. Between the organization of Silver Lake and the first decade of the new century, new churches sprung up in virtually every small town—and between the towns—along the Minnesota-Iowa border. Distinctive white steeples suddenly dotted the landscape. As you guided horse and buggy down the dirt roads into town, every second, third or fourth mile a white clapboard Lutheran church— first the solitary building, later the ubiquitous cemetery with black iron fencing—came into view. Four of these churches were Lime Creek, Emmons, Trinity, and Bethlehem Lutheran.

The Boxes gave us some of the particulars. By 1870, a cluster of Norwegian immigrant families living near Lime Creek on the Minnesota-Iowa border were meeting regularly for Sunday services. An ordained minister from Silver Lake, forty-plus miles to the south, came every couple of months to administer the Eucharist, baptize babies, and do whatever their lay leaders weren't qualified to do. Lay leaders included *klokker* and *skolelerer*. The *klokker* (sexton, parish clerk) was an obvious necessity for rural churches without individual pastors. *Klokkerer* served even into the twentieth century as salaried assistants to a pastor. *Skolelererer* were laypeople hired to teach—confirmation preparation classes for sure, sometimes other religious class as well, and not infrequently also reading, writing, and arithmetic.

It wasn't enough. As population grew, folks yearned for smaller, centralized congregations they could call their own. At Lime Creek, negotiations began to call a real minister. Funds were solicited to put up a building. In 1873 ground was broken on a plot of land on the Minnesota side of what would become Stateline Road; their first pastor arrived two years later. In Emmons, a tiny town three miles east, also on the border, townsfolk soon wanted their own congregation too. A building fund was established. Meanwhile, due west, in the countryside near Bricelyn, Minnesota, farm families organized themselves into Trinity Lutheran. Their building was completed and ready for worship services by mid-1880s. Across the border in Iowa, Lutherans in Buffalo Center formed Bethlehem. They built in 1890.

With all the new congregations and new buildings, Lutheran Ladies Aids *had* to follow. It was inevitable. There was work to be done, and someone needed to do it. By 1874, a dozen Lime Creek Lutheran Church women were meeting regularly, crowded into members' modest parlors in inclement weather and outside in good. In Emmons the Ladies Aid formed several years before the congregation was organized. At Trinity, when by 1887 there was still no Ladies Aid, Pastor Emil Christenson, ignoring doubts from certain members about the wisdom of a women's group, twisted the metaphorical arm of an unmarried lady, one Larsine Hauge, until she finally agreed to invite a dozen women to an informational forum to discuss a *kvindeforening* (women's organization). A year later in Buffalo Center—where the Ladies Literary Circle already held regular meetings— Bethlehem Lutheran began forming its Ladies Aid.

Inevitable as it was, it was also against odds. That the women should be called upon to take up new responsibilities—fundraising, meal planning, janitoring, teaching, giving aid; in short, virtually everything that keeps a congregation going (except preaching and decision-making)—was daunting. There was no telephone service. There was no electricity, no indoor plumbing, no running water; housework was of itself a rather hard slog. On the farm, outside chores, both seasonal and year-round, were added. Transportation was slow and arduous, especially in winter, and winter here could last eight, even nine months. Expecting women to run the church as well was a big imposition.

Even so, by all accounts, women were eager to take on the challenge. Perhaps they saw it as a way to influence a congregation (only male congregants voted or held office). They must have seen it as a means to socialize (life on the prairie could be lonesome). According to L. DeAn Lagerquist (*In America the Men Milk the Cows*, p. 148) the impetus to form a women's group was invariably financial, and perhaps it was. However, more than any other reason, undoubtedly, they saw *kvindeforening* as a way to serve.

Not everyone welcomed organized Ladies Aids. Opposition came in the form of fear, voiced and unvoiced, about what might happen when women gather together. Voting members of a congregation (men) sometimes thought the formation of a women's organization new, radical, and even dangerous. "Whispers persisted that these groups actually served as a cover to promote 'women's rights propaganda'" ("Threads in Women's Hands," Susan Wilds McArver, *Lutheran Women Today*, Jan /Feb 2005). One reason pastors began routinely attending *kvindeforening* meetings was to monitor what was said, find out who and what were prayed for, learn what project plans were discussed, and influence where any monies raised would be directed. Sometimes opposition even came from women themselves, although "resistance" might be a more apt term. A story is told in the Trinity history—the same one Gwen typed for her mother—that an unnamed man forced his wife to go to the women's group against her wishes, and "to her husband's joy, [she] came home with a new conception of the Ladies Aid," becoming a faithful member who "spun and knitted at home unceasingly, never tired of working for the Lord." In spite of opposition, the women congregated. Ladies Aid *was* inevitable. And once organized, everyone came. Lime Creek's *kvindeforening* became so large and spread out over such distances that it quickly organized itself into numbers one and two, then added three and four.

THE *KVINDEFORENINGER*

The more Ann and I talked with Gwen and Vi and the other Ladies about these early history matters, the more confused we became. For starters, their language included names and terms that, although we might have heard before, we needed to fully understand. Time for yet another session with Alma, Marita, and Linnea in the library. They were patient teachers.

We read that in finding the need to organize a women's group, Lutheran women of the region weren't alone. Beginning with the Civil War when women's groups were formed to aid relief efforts, the movement spread rapidly across the nation—church groups, service societies, civic clubs, sororities and social organizations, craft guilds, even political organizations emerged everywhere, many taking on the title "ladies aid" without any church affiliation, years before Norwegian Lutheran women in America would call themselves that. For better or worse, the Victorian Era had brought with it the four-pronged cult of domesticity: piety, purity, submissiveness, and domesticity (or service). A Ladies Aid could fulfill each standard. Bible study taught piety and purity; submissiveness and service would naturally follow.

From a contemporary vantage point, we tend to identify early Norwegian Lutheran women's organizations by the term "Ladies Aid." It wasn't, however, the appellation they gave themselves. They were, as noted, *kvindeforeninger* (*kvinde* [women] and *forening* [association]). Members were mostly first and second generation immigrants, having arrived from Norway by waves in the 1840s, 1860s and 1880s. Almost all spoke native Norwegian. They struggled to integrate Old Country ways into their new lives. After they formed, a fourth wave of immigrants joined them at the turn of the century, reinforcing native language and customs. Within the membership in these early days, every woman could recount the story of immigration. That story was so much a part of their lives that even those too young to remember the Atlantic passage or those actually born in America felt they'd lived it: weathering the crossing, landing on America's eastern shore or in Canada, migrating to Ohio or Wisconsin, then finally going on to join relatives in the prairies and Great Plains. Minnesota's and Iowa's rich soils and supporting (albeit severe) weather welcomed them.

The greatest portion settling in Minnesota and Iowa were farmers. They had come from farming stock in Norway, where they'd most likely lived on a *tun*, a sort of small, collective farming unit, sometimes a family, sometimes parts of different families. In the Old Country, they were of the lowest economic standing and class, and there had been little opportunity to better themselves. For most that was an important reason for immigration. In America things were reputed to be different. And they were. Fluid social and economic structures allowed people to move from one stratus to another. Frequently and conveniently, what was brought from the lower class in Norway could be turned on its head, Americanized into something quite different. Two examples include food and language. For instance, *lutefisk*—the fish of the poor in Norway— was elevated to elegant holiday fare. In language the inversion can be illustrated by the word *mor* (mother). Here in America it was raised to a term of respect and endearment for a married woman, and *bestemor* (grandmother) was the parallel for an elderly woman. In Norway, a woman from the elite class was addressed as *frue*; in middle class, she was *madam*; only in the lowest class was she *mor*. Of course, very few *frue*s or *madam*s chose to immigrate.

Often Alma, Marita, and Linnea took us back to the Old Country. Replete in a settler's memory was the Norwegian State Church. The Lutheran church as state church had been established in 1537 during a period when Norway was part of Denmark. The Sabbath Observance laws of 1735 made the rite of confirmation (at approximately age fifteen) mandatory; six years later in 1741 the Conventicle Act forbade sectarian religious meetings and made strict proscriptions for spiritual practice. The government kept a tight rein on religious life. Economic life and political life were similarly regulated. As far as social life, the class you belonged to dictated roles for men and women in both public and private life.

Much of the immigrants' understanding about what it meant to be Lutheran can be attributed to two individuals, Erik Pontoppidan and Hans Nielsen Hauge. Pontoppidan was an eighteenth century bishop from Bergen. His *Truth unto Godliness, an Explanation of Luther's Small Catechism* was the definitive handbook for Lutheran confirmation in Norway. First published in 1738, Pontoppidan's *Explanation* came with immigrants to

America; in 1842 it was reprinted in New York. The original *Explanation* consisted of 759 questions and answers that confirmands were expected to memorize, although by the mid-eighteenth century the number had been revised down to 451. Whether or not confirmands in America, and especially in the Lime Creek Synod, ever actually memorized all 451 is unclear, but women confirmed after 1930, including our Ladies, remember standing in front of the congregation and being quizzed by their pastors several times during their two or three years of study. Ellen, for instance, who was confirmed at Lime Creek Lutheran in the '30s, reiterates the experience of many. "It had to be letter-perfect, word for word. You might miss one, but if you missed two, your name would go right up on the chart where everyone could see it. Everyone would know you'd failed. Oh, that was a terrible punishment! I suppose if you did that now someone would cry abuse," she says.

The second influential person was Hans Nielsen Hauge, a revivalist on the heels of Pontoppidan. Among other reform measures, Hauge stressed the importance of literacy for Norwegians, ostensibly so that the two most important books in the Norwegian language, Pontoppidan's *Explanation* and the Bible, were accessible to all. Hauge's zeal over teaching the populace to read was such that his followers were called *lesere* (readers). The Ladies remember that their parents and grandparents spoke of Hauge almost in the same breath as Martin Luther. When we asked during interviews what women remembered about Pontoppidan, they gave us mostly blank stares. "It's Hauge that we looked to; we were Haugean Lutherans," said Vi. "Well, I think there's a Pontoppidan church somewhere out in the Dakotas. A school too maybe, but nothing here."

THE NATIONAL CLIMATE

If the State church in Norway had seemed repressive, at least it had held disagreements at bay. Not so in America. Here what it meant to be Lutheran could be interpreted in a variety of ways. That Lutheran immigrants identified themselves as Haugeans was sure; however, how to live out Haugian Lutheranism was up for debate. Would a Haugien do this or that? Decide a political issue for the right or left? Train children by rote or by reason and experience? How often to celebrate the Eucharist? What was the role of women? How should a pastor be called? What is the proper relationship between church and politics? Upon arriving in the New World, strong-willed immigrants (are there any other kind?) allowed the proliferation of positions to multiply and flourish. By the late 1800's, several synods, each with its own specific spin, had emerged. It was as if the journey across the Atlantic allowed the floodgates of passion and opinion to open, as Lagerquist says. Thus, a proliferation of synods. Leading up to 1930, a partial list included the Joint Synod of Ohio, the Lutheran Free Church, General Federation of the Iowa Synod, the Buffalo Synod, United Lutheran Church, American Lutheran Church, Evangelical Lutheran Church, United Evangelical Lutheran Church, American Evangelical Lutheran Church, and the Suomi Synod and their corresponding women's organizations (or lack thereof). Most had grown out of the earlier-organized General Synod in Pennsylvania. It was enough to make your head swim.

By 1930 the Norwegian Evangelical Lutheran Church had emerged from several smaller synods coming together, and its membership included 90% of the Norwegian Lutherans living in America. As mentioned earlier, the years between 1930 and 1960 were not chosen arbitrarily. 1930 ushered in a three-decade era of stability between mergers. Besides synodic calm, several other factors led to a suitable environment for women's growth. First, the quadricentennial anniversary of Luther's Ninety-five Theses in 1917 produced large celebrations with cooperation among the various Lutheran groups to observe their common identity (*The Lutherans*, Lagerquist). Second, national women's suffrage was accomplished with the ratification of the Nineteenth Amendment in 1920. Though individual churches might not sanction women's participation in leadership or voting for several more years, the fact that they now had a voice nationally influenced the way women thought about themselves. Third, that same year the Women's Missionary Federation of the Lutheran Church was founded. The WMF provided individual congregations with a large, supportive body for guidance, as well as a channel into which they could reliably funnel their resources. Membership in the WMF connected local women with world-wide missions. And fourth, a year later Congress passed the Johnson-Reed Act restricting immigration. Known as the Quota Act, it insured that from that moment on, new Lutherans in America would have to come from within the country, not from overseas (Lagerquist). These four things intensified a need for Lutherans to develop into a church with American identity, in time distancing Norwegian Americans from the land of their ancestry.

Outside the Norwegian Lutheran community, certain other developments contributed to an environment that made it easier for women to congregate. In 1930, the national census revealed that one in five Americans owned an automobile. Electricity was becoming more readily available. The Rural Electric Association wasn't established until 1935, but prior to that, power could be obtained through the installation of a Delco plant (a sort of large, re-chargeable battery) in a home or other facility. Several of the Ladies remember the Delco plant's bing-bing-bing that accompanied their basement meetings.

And then the Great Depression hit. That brought a reason—a *need*—for people to come together, a need to support each other. If in 1930, a fifth of adult Americans owned an automobile, a year later the stock market crashed, leaving many of those autos to rust in farmyards. Banks dissolved, and panic ensued. Unemployment was estimated between four and five million. By 1933, 2000 rural schools had closed, leaving 200,000 teachers out of work and 2.3 million students at home. Women needed a place where they could find solace and solidarity, a place where they could help each other out and give to the wider community. The Ladies Aid provided exactly that. Bringing practicality to their common cause assuaged a growing dread.

1930: The Ladies Aid Meeting

Ask Alma, Marita, and Linnea and they'll tell you that national economics, industrial improvements, celebrations, and Congressional acts aside, perhaps the single most important development of all when it came to encouraging active Ladies Aids in the '30s was: the church basement. A basement provided a place for work and social gatherings. The basement gave a space for a central heating plant, meeting rooms, classrooms, library, storage, bathroom facilities, and—most importantly—a kitchen. Prior to the addition of a basement, church women's groups met in homes in inclement weather or out under the trees in summertime if the group was too large for a home. (One interesting exception is the case of Emmons where historical records reveal that the *kindnerforingen*'s first meeting place was upstairs over the local hardware store.) Basements at all four of our church buildings were added in the '20's. Although no records remain of council conversations pertaining to basement planning, it would be interesting to eavesdrop on those sessions!

From the beginning, the typical meeting was day-long. Even with improved transportation and a central meeting place guaranteed to be warm and dry, the tradition of the day-long meeting held. There was much to do. By now attendance had blossomed to include virtually every adult female in the congregation. Two or three women hostessed the monthly meeting. Ten or fifteen cents was charged per meal (an increase to twenty-five cents in the mid-'40s caused controversy in all the congregations!). Lunch typically consisted of creamed chicken on toast, pickles, salad (Jello), and cake (white with lemon filling). Five hours later, supper would probably be meatloaf, mashed potatoes, and a vegetable, plus dessert. The beverage of choice was always coffee, preferably Scandinavian egg coffee, so tricky to make that in at least one congregation, the coffeemaker—Carrie—was the only woman on actual payroll. Supper was a large crowd: husbands, businessmen from town, school teachers, and often children attended. Ten cents, fifteen cents, even twenty-five cents was a bargain for a good, filling meal.

The pastor came to give devotions. A meeting wasn't a meeting without a pastor. The women wanted his presence to legitimize things; the men wanted the pastor present to control things. In either case, his spiritual and intellectual leadership was highly coveted and rarely questioned. Although the officers might run things, surely his presence was necessary to put a stamp of importance and permission on everything. So important did a pastor take this responsibility that one retired minister tells how after his first child was born, when the date of an Aid meeting coincided with picking up his wife from the hospital, he went from hospital directly to Aid with wife and newborn son in tow!

Church was the number one social outlet beyond family and immediate neighborhood. A town's social organizations—women's literary clubs or 4-H for the youth, both of which were already active in Buffalo Center by this time—had to vie for membership attention from church.

We asked Alma, Marita, and Linnea to describe Ladies Aid members in 1930, and they eagerly complied. Their stories are representative—indistinguishable from those of our own mother, aunts, and the rest of the Ladies

"I was a hired girl; so was my sister." Alma's aunt had five children, all under the age of eight. "One winter she became ill—pneumonia, I suppose, or something like that—and there was no way she could do her housework and care for those babies. I was sixteen so I was sent to help. And when she was well, I stayed. When I graduated from high school, my sister took over." Many of the Ladies had been hired girls for aunts or neighbors. Being a hired girl was training ground, certainly not a mark of poverty or degradation. Teenaged girls often spent their summers at the job, and occasionally their placements continued in after hours throughout the school year. Girls without plans for post-high school education often bided their time between schooling and marriage as hired girls.

Most of the Ladies had high school degrees; some would have had secretarial, nursing, or normal training besides. Marita had secretarial training. "Oh, yes; the message in my family was always 'You might have a husband, but what happens if your husband gets ill or dies?' So even we girls wanted some sort of education beyond high school." In actuality, in this rural setting, more girls than boys were sent off for higher education; boys could more easily find work in farming or manufacturing, both of which had on-the-job training.

Many were farm wives with the usual housework, plus gardening of fruits and vegetables, canning, butchering and meat processing, field work, feeding of livestock, milking, sewing clothing, and food preparation for seasonal work crews (threshing in the fall, for instance). "Well, the threshing crew!" remembered Linnea. "They'd come through every fall, a dozen or so men. They'd be a week on this farm, a week on the next. Imagine twelve extra men crowded around your table at every meal."

The women had also begun to think of themselves differently. The wave of American nationalism that developed after World War I and the urge to be identified as American rather than Norwegian are factors that moved an individual congregation to transform its women's organization from "*kvindeforening*" to a Ladies Aid. However, Norwegian heritage still colored and enriched lives. They might be Americans, but they didn't want anybody to forget that the *best* Americans (and the best Lutherans) came from Norway. The Ladies remembered *klokkerer* and *skolelererer* from their youth. For many, baptism and confirmation would have been in the Norwegian language, including memorization of the Haugean version of Luther's Small Catechism.

Native languages, after all, are more than identity. They are also the core of spiritual relationship. Many of the Ladies remembered some of the Norwegian language. Hermoine relates that at Trinity, even as late as the '50s children were taught the Ten Commandments, at least one Christmas carol, and the Lord's Prayer in Norwegian, as well as the traditional table grace and John 3:16. "We were hedging our bets against a God who might still speak Norwegian!" she laughs.

Hermoine's words make Ann and me think about our own Grandma Clara. Technically speaking, she was English-speaking, not Nordic-speaking. However, there were a myriad of ways that the Norwegian language still influenced her life. It was more than the speaking of the language; it was the knowledge and acceptance of the language as an easy and useful way of communicating. Grandma wrote in Norwegian to her relatives in Norway in Lapland. She and Grandpa used it periodically at home. She read it. So she was fluent, but it wasn't her everyday language as it had been for her parents.

It was reserved for special occasions and special people. To use it on the street with a friend was like affirming that they both belonged to the same secret organization; they shared secret knowledge. She also used it to keep information away from her children—discussing discipline with Grandpa, disagreeing with Grandpa, talking about adult topics, or telling Christmas secrets.

To use it in special occasions kept it akin to holiness, separate from the vernacular. Only special church services were spoken in the language, mostly holiday celebrations. Children were taught the holiest of passages: the Lord's Prayer, Christmas hymns, the Ten Commandments. And the daily table prayer for mealtimes. Our mother remembered learning the mealtime prayer and a bedtime prayer as well.

Sometimes language revealed Grandma's ambivalence. We never heard her use the word "husband," only "man." *Mann* is Norwegian for husband. We knew when we heard her call our grandfather "my man" that she was talking about someone special. Grandma also used the Nordic expression that has become in recent years a humorous signal for Nordic ancestry: *ufftah*. Good Lutherans didn't say *gee* or *golly* or *darn*, let alone anything stronger. Ufftah was just about the only expletive allowed. She said it over things that might be confusing or difficult or mildly disturbing.

If something made her particularly angry, it got lengthened to *ufftah-feedah*. And on the rare occasion we heard "*ufftah-feedah-MAI!*" we knew we were in trouble.

Grandma would have been forty years old in 1930 when our mother was ten. So complete was the Americanization of Mom's generation that an understanding of vernacular Norwegian had been totally lost. Mom didn't even have an interest in learning it. Another difference between the generations was evident in the amount of communication with Norway. Whereas Grandma regularly corresponded with her cousins in Lapland and Stavenger, Mom had no connection.

Grandma Clara and her friends brought all their assumed Norwegian-ness along to Ladies Aid. Ann and I don't need Alma, Marita, and Linnea to help us envision the Ladies' meetings—we simply recall Grandma's stories. A hypothetical Aid meeting in 1930 meant giving up an entire day after having spent some hours the day before in preparation, but it was a social highlight and well worth the effort. Except for Sundays, it would be quite usual not to see other women for weeks at a time. Lime Creek Ladies Aid met on the first Wednesday of each month. By this time Grandma had eight children ranging in age from sixteen to three years. At fourteen, Eunice was the oldest girl, old enough to be an effective babysitter for her siblings, but still a little young for being a hired girl. In the summertime, Grandma could easily count on Eunice to watch the children for a day. But let's say that this particular meeting happens in November, and Eunice and all but Helen the toddler are in school for the day. Already the snow has begun to fly; almost a foot covers the landscape. On this Wednesday morning, Buell, the oldest, hitches one of the two farm horses to the buckboard, and the kids pile in among blankets for their two-mile ride up the dirt county road to school.

Meanwhile, Grandpa has warmed up the Model T. Grandma packs her sewing, a couple of extra loaves of bread, two jars of jam, and Helen into the car, and they set off for the church. Along the way, they collect aunts

Gertrude, Julia, and Tillie and assorted babies plus a couple other neighborhood women. Not sharing our modern need for seatbelts, they could pack a lot of people in, and the women didn't mind occupying a lap for short rides. (As children, whenever we'd complain about not having enough room in the car, Mom would relate the story of traveling between Minnesota and South Dakota on summer vacations with eleven people in the car, sitting "one-up-one-back" across bench seats.) At each collection, Grandma and Grandpa call out "*Godt dag, godt dag!*" and "*Hvordan stor til!*" which are returned with "*Ja sa godt! Et tu?*"

An hour later, they arrive at Lime Creek. The Ladies unpack the car and themselves. Grandpa unlocks the church door for them, assures them he'll be back with the children in time for supper, and then leaves to return home to his work. The Ladies set to work in the frigid basement, first stoking the furnace, then laying out equipment for food preparation. By the time the rest of the membership arrives an hour later, the air is warm and the coffee is boiling. They're ready for festivities to begin.

CHAPTER THREE
ORGANIZING UNDER THE
WOMEN'S MISSIONARY FEDERATION

Friends, there is something brewing in my mind—something new among our people. Mr. Dahl is the only one I have mentioned it to. He thinks it would be a fine thing. I feel our women should begin to plan for a mission federation. What other denominations are doing, we can do for the grace of God.
            —Rebecca Dahl, first president, Women's Missionary Federation

Linnea has organizational sense and a political mind. Every Aid had to have a Linnea. At Trinity, her name was Hermoine.

What Hermoine and the Linneas of the world have is the ability to envision how individual organizational systems work in and of themselves—one specific Ladies Aid, for instance, with its board of officers and smaller divisions called "circles"—and how that system is connected to and benefits from membership in a larger body, in this case, the Women's Missionary Federation.

By the time Hermoine joined Trinity's Ladies Aid, the relationship with the WMF was solid. The WMF had come into being in 1911 and was headquartered in St. Paul, Minnesota. Its formation is attributed in great part to one Rebecca Dahl who had for years dreamed of a church organization that could unite all Lutheran women. Mrs. Dahl became the WMF's first president. It in turn was divided into districts; Trinity dealt directly with the district office in Minneapolis. Across what was once the vast

Silver Lake Synod, many of the Ladies, like Gwen and Vi, were here because they were born here. Not so with Hermoine. She came to Trinity the way many of today's women end up where they are, because her job brought her. Hermoine joined Trinity when she was hired to teach home economics in the local high school. During her tenure she held almost every Aid office possible. And beyond. She enjoyed knowing something about the big picture. She had good organizational structure. She liked being in positions that made a difference. For all those reasons, she volunteered year after year as delegate to the district meetings. For all those reasons, and because it was fun. "I so enjoyed meeting women from all over. There were always important women at those district conventions and you got to hear about new ideas and what was happening at every level and how your congregation's Ladies Aid was going to be affected. And you got to feel like you were really making a difference," she said. "Whatever the discussion, I wanted to understand it and I wanted people to know my opinion."

From our first visit with Hermoine it was clear that she had her finger on the pulse of Trinity. She knew something about everyone and everything. But when we asked her to talk about how Trinity ran under the WMF, she demurred. "If you want to understand how our Aid works organizationally, you should get to know Gwen and Vi. Yes, they'd be the exact people to talk to. Gwen can tell you lots of Trinity history, the kinds of things I don't know because I didn't have ancestors here. And Vi is just such a worker!" And so off we went to find Gwen and Vi.

The Local Chapter

"Growing up, I always knew that Ladies Aid, that going to Ladies Aid, was important." Vi recalls her personal church history. "I was baptized by an old pastor. Really old. Xavier was his name. *Zavee-ay* was how you'd pronounce it, even though it started with an X. He was a pastor who came to our church, and then they were asking who's the oldest and how many years have you been here, and things like that, and I said I was baptized by Xavier," she tells us. "Of course, I had heard it so many times. You don't remember when you were baptized."

She does, however, remember the beginnings of her life in the Ladies Aid. "I was married at Trinity. It rained, oh my, it rained. We picked the first of April. It was my birthday. But it worked out fine. We've been married 62 years. And then once I was married, it was just expected that I went to Aid." A life-long member of Trinity, Vi had been active in Luther League as a teenager, then active in the Lutheran Daughters of the Reformation (LDR) as a young unmarried woman. Usually once a woman was married, expectations for membership transferred from the LDR to Ladies Aid.

What was it like for Vi to attend her first Aid meeting? To join? What would she have been expected to know? To do? According to Trinity's historical records from The Box, in 1942—the year of Vi's marriage—there were 43 members listed on the Ladies Aid roster, with 13 officers, as prescribed by the by-laws: President, Vice President, Secretary, and Treasurer; Secretaries of Mission Box, Thank-offering, In Memoriam, Box (separate from Mission Box), Flower Fund, Mowing Fund, and Cradle Roll; plus Historian and Librarian. There were also three committees, each with a minimum of two chairwomen: Serving, Sewing, and Membership. Nineteen jobs to be filled. Records from the following year show that three additional offices were added—Secretaries of Membership, Christian Nurture, and Pew Fund—plus a Kitchen Committee. In 1944, Secretaries of Organ Fund and Self Denial are listed as well. Amazingly, for all three of those years, no one was duplicated in the lists: every office had at least one elected official (in some instances two women shared an office), and no one held more than one position. That made the ratio of offices to general membership almost one to one.

In each list, names of members and officers are given in full—albeit by husbands' names. In a sense, that was elevation. Marriage was preferable to being single; singles rarely held office past their Luther League and LDR days. To be married and listed as such was a badge of honor, a rite of passage into complete womanhood. A husband's name lent import, credibility, and maturity to a woman. Between '42 and '44, only two women are listed as "Miss."

One gets the feeling that recording the specific duties of each office wasn't as important as naming the person who held the office. People, not rules and regulations, were the focus of Ladies Aid. While year by year the officers are painstakingly recorded, the nature of each office isn't so clear. We can infer what sorts of duties the president, vice president, secretary, and treasurer would have had, but it's a bit harder to imagine over half a century later the duties of Box Secretary or Secretary of Self Denial. Perhaps both the general membership and the historian took these duties for granted and felt no need to describe them.

Membership in the Aid implied at least five things. First and second were the expectation of regular attendance at every meeting and the payment of dues. Meetings were held once or twice a month, depending on holidays and summertime. The Treasurer called roll, appropriate since proof of attendance was recorded by dues' collection, something common to all four of our congregations. Through the three decades, the amount expected fluctuated between five and twenty-five cents, but there was no question about paying it. "At the beginning," reads Trinity's history, "it was decided to meet twice a month and charge a fee of ten cents payable at every other meeting. They had roll call and each member paid her ten cents. If her name was given and she were not there, an 'X' would be put in front of her name and she would pay it the next time they met."

Trinity wasn't alone. Organization was similar in other Aids. At Emmons, Ellen (a sort of Alma-Marita-Linnea combination) says, "They did call roll, and it was unusual not to be there. My mother was treasurer [Lime Creek, the '30's], and she had to call roll. They called roll at every meeting. You couldn't do that any more. You'd have a lot of silence." She remembers [Emmons, the '50's] "some little squabbles" about it from time to time. "One would say, 'I can remember being there,' and the other would say, 'No, you weren't,' and 'Well, yes, I was.' For a quarter! It'd be easier to throw a quarter at them than haggle about it! You had to pay up. You were *supposed* to pay up. After all, it was money for missions and the like."

Third, membership automatically implied an understanding of responsibilities. These weren't the duties expected from officers—which would be listed in by-laws and could be read by anyone elected to a position—but were rather the kinds of understood activities of any organization which evolves organically through successive generations. They included participation in all extra events, a reasonable standard of craft production, and contributing to general meetings through serving lunch, acting as scripture readers, or planning/presenting programs, each on a regular rotational basis. Performance of these activities was the kind of thing that could mark you as derelict if you didn't anticipate it. Exceptions were rare, as evidenced by recording them in Aid histories. For instance, Trinity notes in the '40's that "Mrs. F. donated $25 instead of serving." In 1942, that was a substantial sum. About Emmons, Ellen comments, "Everyone was pretty willing to serve, to bring a pan of bars or whatnot. And you kind of knew who wasn't, and you'd skip them because it's not worth the effort." In all the congregations, women over 70 were no longer *required* to serve food; they could pay [normally $3] instead of baking or cooking.

One could wonder why Mrs. F.'s refusal to serve got herself recorded into written history. More common was that the woman who didn't understand or didn't follow the "rules" was turned into the subject of anecdote. We chuckled at the story of one lady who was famous for her potato salad, but not in a good way. Whenever it appeared—apparently frequently—every effort was made to spirit it away from the serving table. This was long before the days of garbage disposals. Once the serving team resorted to flushing it down the toilet. That, however, increased the problem when she discovered her salad had disappeared before anyone else's.

Like Gwen and Vi, many Aid members simply inherited the knowledge of their duties. Again and again we heard "my mother was president/secretary/treasurer," and each time the interviewee was a woman who had held multiple offices herself. Even so, Gwen recalls how as an LDR Girl, she was never expected to give a devotional or Bible lesson, whereas upon becoming a Ladies Aid member, she was listed in the written program for "Devotions" at her very first meeting. "I just copied all my years of sitting under Sunday school teachers," she said.

Another Lady told us that on moving to Trinity, she soon learned she'd been added to the roster for a certain committee, but not until she'd unwittingly missed the first meeting. To add insult to injury, the committee had been organized to knit sweaters for missions, and she didn't knit.

Fourth, you were expected occasionally to give The Program. Meetings usually consisted of singing a hymn, listening to a devotional reading, praying, going through an abbreviated Roberts-Rules-of-Order business format, and The Program. The Program was a topical presentation, often listed by title in the yearbook a year in advance. When you were listed as responsible for The Program you could choose to present it yourself or organize others to give it. As Ellen reports, "We received very good materials once a month." These were from the WMF who provided regular news of national causes and international missions and sometimes written materials or presentations. Or you could look locally for something or someone who matched your assigned theme. Something seasonal was always appropriate. Local personages or scholars could be invited to share their experiences. A look through Bethlehem's yearbooks of the '30s reveals several recurrent, topical celebrations as programs. History Day each April honored charter members. September meetings were designated as Mission Days. Ellen says you were especially lucky if you could recruit "missionaries home from the mission field. They were so very interesting." On Guest Day members were encouraged to invite non-church women to attend, and a local celebrity was invited to speak. Other regular program listings were the annual Thank Offering and Self Denial Days. Once a year the identity, composition, or workings of the WMF itself was featured, as when Bethlehem noted "Playlet on WMF" as the program of the day with a listing of cast members; but, sadly, no script remains.

Fifth, every member needed to be willing and able to hold elected office. Executive offices—president, vice president, treasurer, and secretary—would have been written into the constitution, both duties and language being provided by the national Women's Missionary Federation. Other offices, the "secretaries" of various duties, grew out of local need and were listed in by-laws. Generally speaking, the WMF template provided leadership for a smooth-running organization.

One complication to orderliness arose when congregations fell under two-point and sometimes even three-point designations, when a single pastor was shared by more than one congregation. Such was the case for Lime Creek and Emmons. From "The History of Lime Creek Church" recorded in the early '40s, we read:

> In 1919 the South Aid joined the WMF, and in 1920 the North Aid joined. During this period, there have been two separate organizations, except on special occasions such as bazaars and suppers, which they held once a year, or when they served together for mission meetings.

During these early years when horses rather than autos served as primary transportation, even the distance of three miles was significant. By the '30s, things were different. "In 1934, after several attempts, they united into one Ladies Aid and adopted the proposed constitution of the WMF." "One Ladies Aid," however, was easier said than done. Where would the meetings be held? If in Emmons, Lime Creek women would have to drive further to attend; but if at Lime Creek, *everyone* would have to drive since the building was out in the country. Alternating by months, by seasons, and by six-month intervals were all tried. Finally, a compromise was reached. They shared one constitution but elected separate officers, coming together for special meetings and holiday celebrations.

CIRCLES

One organizational structure where distance was rarely a problem was the circle. Members were assigned to circles or study groups in each congregation, reminiscent of ancient biblical patterns of apportioning responsibility. Whatever the job—child care during worship, food preparation for special events, housecleaning—the circles took turns. The circle was also a place for Bible training, with regular lessons assigned to meetings. These were often led by the pastor or another specially trained person (often the pastor's wife). Books, lecture series, guest speakers, and other specific study aids were sometimes employed, but circles were more apt to be rather relaxed, without the strictness of regular business meetings and programs. The circle was more personal. This was where best friends could be made, prayer requests circulated, and problems of a more personal nature discussed.

Ann and I had a lot of questions we wanted to ask about circles. How were they formed? Who was assigned to which? How often did they meet? What were their duties, responsibilities, etc.? Did they have officers? One day we went to chat with Pastor Lloyd, long-retired, recently widowed, and making his home in an assisted living facility. We began by telling him that to us, the circle arrangement was reminiscent of ancient Biblical patterns—set forth in the desert wanderings of Exodus—of apportioning responsibility. He was quick to give us his pastoral view: "No such thing at all! Circles were for fun, not for getting the work done!" Fun they had, but the Ladies would still argue his point. We went back to them to get the real story.

Circles were organized for various reasons. Between Lime Creek and Emmons, there were active circles long before the '30s, even before the congregation at Emmons was incorporated. Although named "Aid organizations, Nos. 1-4" they followed both pattern and purposes of circles. In these cases, membership in a circle had more to do with location than anything else. But as family cars proliferated, making transportation less a matter of concern, circles were organized for all manner of reasons. Sometimes a Lady chose her circle; sometimes it was assigned or at least suggested. She might choose because of meeting times, especially when women began joining the professional work force, or because of a social group. Circle populations were apt to form around themes—age, craft interests, mission projects, intellectual study, spiritual pursuits, and friendship. They were usually named after Bible women. "We always had two or three," recalls Trinity's Vi. "We chose if we wanted to be in the day or the morning circle. Ruth, Lois; we had all kinds of names, just so long as they came from the Bible." Besides Ruth and Lois, in our research we found Mary, Mary Magdalene, Martha, Dorcas, Esther, Deborah, Miriam, Sarah, Rebekkah, Rachel, Elizabeth, and Anna. There were notably no Delilahs, Bathshebas, or Judiths—and no Eves (because of that thing she had with the serpent?) and no Leahs (too weak-eyed?).

Although we couldn't find documents to pin it down, *everyone* knew what a circle was for. Much must have been intuited. Some specific uses our women talked about were:

- to apportion housekeeping jobs,
- to apportion secretarial jobs,
- to apportion worship-related assignments,
- for Bible training,
- to socialize,
- to raise money for missions,
- for the dissemination of information,
- to apportion job responsibilities for congregation-wide events,
- to be more open, more inclusive, more relaxed, and less formal than the larger Ladies Aid. To this end, circles were often open to outsiders, women not members of the congregation, women not necessarily Lutheran, sometimes not members of any church.

Ellen told us that "circles included everyone. Catholics? Everyone. Outsiders could belong to a circle. They were a sort of separate organization. They weren't asked to do things by the church like they are now, to do this, that, and the other thing."

DISTRICTS, CIRCUITS, SYNODS, AND CONVENTIONS

"Well, I remember going to different meetings at different churches, even Minneapolis one time. I sure remember that one because it was the day I was going to quit drinking coffee. It didn't work! I guess you need coffee to get through those meetings!" Vi is recalling her experiences when she served on the district council. Individual congregations were assigned to a larger district or circuit.

In records preserved in The Boxes, we found the terms "district" and "circuit" frequently interchanged, but when we wondered if they were in fact the same, Hermoine set us straight. A circuit included the churches in the immediate vicinity. We were reminded of Lime Creek's early days with its circuit-riding pastor whose churches were never more than a day's horse ride apart. "The circuit was about twelve to thirteen churches in the area. The district was bigger—like the Southern Minnesota District." Circuit gatherings were held a couple of times a year. "They were always much more interesting than the district. The circuits were all small churches, country churches like ours. Some bigger ones—whichever were in that particular area."

A board of officers was nominated and elected from Ladies Aids within the circuit. There was a business meeting where policy decisions were made and information from the district disseminated. Usually a district officer would be in attendance. Some policy decisions were made, and a program was presented.

"And we always had a circuit chorus. We had so much wonderful music!" Hermoine sang not only in Trinity's choir, but in both circuit and district choruses as well. "For years Screwball Nelson, the old baseball player, directed. He had such a thick Norwegian accent and a big, booming voice. I remember once he exhorted us to 'Sing it yust like it's vritten in the book: Now Tank Ve All our Godt!' and we all got the giggles so bad we could hardly sing!"

"Well, we didn't have TV in those days—so we had more music. Your social life got to be the church, or the school. Very different from today. It's changed. Everything changes, and it's not all bad. Just different," Hemoine observed.

Congregations hosted circuit and district meetings, and each of our Ladies Aids took their turns. Other years they faithfully sent delegates. Bethlehem's Box tells us that in 1938 and '39 the Ladies Aid sent two delegates each to Lost Island (Waterloo), Doliver, Cylinder, and Milfred, all part of the Estherville Circuit in north central Iowa, and another two delegates to MWF conventions (district) in Northwood, Iowa, and Mankato, Minnesota. Perhaps all that driving prepared them for the following year: The Box also tells us, "1940: the Aid is using WMF Tour around the World topics for programs."

By the late '50s, there were better roads and better cars, but even so, a day or overnight trip to "convention" was still exciting. "The conventions were good. I enjoyed them. You found out a lot about what the church was doing, where they were heading, what they were trying to improve," remembers Hermoine. "Once, on the first day, I made a mistake and sat in the back of the room. I didn't know any better. Well, in the back of the room everyone sat and visited—they met their sister from the East Coast or a friend from the West—and they're laughing and chatting and having a good time. I learned if you want to hear anything you have to move up to the front of the room."

"Well, I also went to the last one in 1959 before the merger," she recalls. "I was a delegate to Minneapolis. They were talking about the merger. The president of the women of the church made a mistake. She said, 'we're waiting for a word on the *murder* of the church!' Everyone got a pretty good laugh out of that. Probably the way she felt!"

The circuit, the way it was, is gone now.

It was the last time we saw Hermoine. We'd talked about many things in our afternoon together, our families, our shared Norwegian heritage, young women going off to college and older women finding new professions, and, of course, about her first love, the organizational structure of the Ladies Aid within the old WMF. Finally, as we helped her carry coffee cups and plates to the kitchen, we said our goodbyes. She walked us out to the car. We hugged and told her what we said to everyone at the end of an interview, "Call us if you think of anything else!" She put her hands on our shoulders. "Just this one thing: it's changed. Everything changes. And that's not bad. But it's *different*."

CHAPTER FOUR
LUTEFISK OG LEFSE, TAKK SKAL DU HAR

Recipe for a Ladies Aid Society
First take a half day off to attend the Deer Creek Valley Women's Missionary
Federation. Then remove all traces of care and anxiety from your brow. Take the
well beaten path to the Parish House door, filling your hearts with sunshine and
your lungs with oxygen. Pour into the Parish House, shaking hands at the same
time. Add to this mixture sociability and habits of industry. Add separately a
moderate amount of business and an equal quantity of pleasure, mixing to the
proper consistency. When these ingredients have simmered down, refreshments may
be thrown in with a relish. Stir in a generous portion of fruit in the shape of coins.
Variety being the spice of life, season to taste. Cover the mass closely with charity,
taking care that no malice gets in. Serve once every month. (Deer Creek Valley
Lutheran Church Cook Book, 1955)

THE KITCHEN IN THE BASEMENT

If there were a Linnea in each group, it was the Almas who accomplished
much of the kitchen work. At Trinity, Vi was certainly an Alma. "Feeding
the people was, and still is, one of the most important works of the
church," says Vi. "I was always good with food. Don't make me run a
meeting; put me in the kitchen. I've been 'Vi' for a long time, but if they've
been gone for a while, they call me Violet. Whichever, they find me in the
kitchen! I'm always in the kitchen. My husband Einer, he got to find that
out pretty easy. If you want to find me, I'm going to be in the kitchen."

In principle, and certainly on paper, men ran the church. Men held council positions, hired the pastor and his assistants, managed the finances, and made whatever decisions needed to be made. For the most part, the sanctuary and the sacristy provided plenty of room for business to be accomplished. For more casual business, there was always the pastor's living room; for private business, the pastor's office. Not so for the work of the women. You can't cook supper in the pews. Thus, the church basement.

We can only surmise how these came about, whose idea they were, what discussions and arguments surrounded the decisions to dig and build, and how the monies were raised to finance them. The Boxes are silent on the particulars. As already mentioned, what we do know is that within thirty years after Emmons, Lime Creek, Buffalo Center, and Trinity erected their white clapboards that held altar and pews, they dug basements. With basements came central furnaces, meeting spaces, the potential for bathrooms...and kitchens.

Perhaps unwittingly, the basement location of the women's work center was reflective of women's positions in the congregation. Convenience placed the church kitchen at the far end of the basement, adjacent to water and heat sources, and that meant they were almost always directly below the altar. In an era when women couldn't serve on a church council, assist at communion, teach, usher, light the candles on the altar before service, or do anything else within male purview, women's work—largely food preparation—was being carried out twelve feet below the "holy of holies."

Anything but holy in appearances, by modern standards, the first rural church kitchens were neither convenient nor attractive. Many had walls of exposed cement or stone, often whitewashed with a coat of enamel to help control dust and reflect what sunlight was let in by narrow casement windows. The coal-burning furnace itself dominated the space, whether it sat center stage or at either end of the structure. Six to eight feet in diameter, almost as tall as the ceiling, it hunkered menacingly. Long, fat ducts like octopus arms carried heat up to the sanctuary. When fully stoked, it crackled and belched, and the fire within glowed red through seams and around the door. Every function of the furnace was rife with black dust, from the load of coal delivered down chute to bin to shoveling the coal into the furnace belly to tracking coal-smudged shoes over the floor. Vi remembers that at Trinity, "The coal bin was right off the kitchen. That wasn't exactly clean."

In the kitchen itself, a cast iron coal- or wood-burning cookstove served for both cooking and baking. On Aid days, it would be filled and lit early in the morning to heat water to scrub down coal-blackened surfaces. If a dinner were planned, the fire could be kept going all day, boiling scrub water, brewing huge urns of coffee, cooking giant kettles of food, and finally heating more water for washing dishes. Between furnace and cook-stove, the kitchen could be near suffocation, even in coldest weather.

Food preparation in such a space was hard physical labor. Wood and coal are heavy. So is water, which had to be carried in from an outside pump. For a Sunday meal, men could sometimes be enlisted to help with the hauling, but for events during the week, they were often unavailable. At Trinity, countertops and flooring were surfaced with linoleum, which— albeit cracked and peeling by the '40s—was probably superior to the cement floors and metal countertops of many rural church kitchens. It seemed, however, that the surfaces themselves harbored dirt. Women worked hard to keep things clean.

As if dirt and heat weren't enough, other things made the atmosphere unpleasant. In most church basements, once indoor plumbing arrived, bathroom facilities—with their inherent traffic, noise, and odors—were located adjacent to and even opening into the kitchen. Some of these early facilities were little more than a nook off the main path with nothing but a fabric curtain to offer privacy. Hermoine remembers, "Besides the bath-room, the only drain was in the middle of the floor. It wasn't a bit sanitary."

There was clutter, too. Cabinets and closets were often later additions, so the first kitchens were repositories for whatever needed storing—folding tables and chairs, extra lumber, boxes of supplies, tools, and janitorial equipment. "Oh, it was awful. And to think ours was better than most!" She was right; Trinity, with its eight Skelgas hot plates (propane burners) and a Nash percolator, was more modern than many.

Regardless of location and limitation, the kitchen was very much reflective of the life of its congregation, and the people who toiled there were quite literally the foundation of the church. Vi remembers what it was like in Trinity's kitchen when she joined the congregation as a young bride. "That great big furnace was in the middle of the dining room at that time—something like what you'd have in school and different places at that time," she nods at us as if we're supposed to remember as well. "There was a man who'd come over and get it all warmed up real early in the morning so it was warm. We congregated around it, you know. It would be warmed up at one side or another, never all the way around, but that was fine. We didn't have electricity, of course. They'd have little light plants that had batteries in there, and you'd hear bing-bing-bing-bing. It was just a good feeling."

The Ladies knew the importance of serving good food. Whether it was for coffee hour after church, a benefit supper to raise money for the building fund, the wedding or funeral of a parishioner, or the annual fall pull-out-all-the-stops *lutefisk* dinner, food was done big, and it was done right. To credit the Ladies with the longevity of their churches, food preparation was, and still is, a key element in accreditation. There is a direct relation between the presence of food and the vitality of a congregation. To Norwegian Lutherans, just as the bread and wine of the sacrament nourishes the soul, the elements in a good *lutefisk* dinner assure the health of a congregation.

The *Lutefisk* Supper

Chief in food preparation was the annual lutefisk supper. Lutefisk dinners have always been big money-makers for Lutheran congregations through-out the upper Midwest where Norwegian ancestry is still celebrated. In 1936 Trinity's Ladies Aid served "a lutefisk and flotegrot supper" for 250 people with proceeds of $89.80. By 1950, the number served had increased to 450, netting $397.73. Even today, people drive two or three hours for a good lutefisk dinner. During the Depression, the cost of a meal might be as low as twenty-five cents; today it's increased to $15 or $20 per meal. With 500 to 1000 diners per event, it's lucrative. It's also labor intensive, and prices are low precisely because labor is not today and never was figured into the dollar cost.

A typical lutefisk dinner began with heaping plates of glutinous white codfish, soaked in water to remove the lye, then carefully boiled to proper consistency. It was a tricky process because if overcooked, lutefisk be-comes nearly liquefied. To lutefisk connoisseurs, the texture was as impor-tant as the taste. To say the least, the dish was odiferous. Memories of a lutefisk dinner lasted several days. Most people ate it with melted butter which enhances the flavor. Not everyone liked the taste, but a lutefisk board groaned with side dishes to please other palates. Along with the fish were unlimited quantities of meatballs and gravy, mashed potatoes, vege-tables, and *lefse*. The meal ended with Scandinavian pastries: *krumkaka*, rosettes, *fatigmann*, and *sandbakkels*.

Why lutefisk? Why an entire fund-raising machine centered around dried cod cured in lye and reconstituted by boiling? "It was something exciting to everyone," says Vi. Lutefisk, imported from Norway, was avail-able mostly at holiday time, and its preparation was work intensive. Aver-age households couldn't afford it, so it became special fare, served with a holiday atmosphere. "Once a year, um hum! Everybody wore fancy aprons, which they don't nowadays. But we got special ones then. Fancy aprons for lutefisk!" Vi chuckles at her memory. Important to Norwegian immigrant heritage, lutefisk, lefse, and other Scandinavian foods are the food of the homeland, and the dinners were (and are) a way to celebrate and preserve tradition. In Norway in the nineteenth century, lutefisk was a staple for the poor. The dried fish could be stored indefinitely, then reconstituted as necessary. On a trip to Norway today, one would be hard pressed to find lutefisk anywhere. The country exports more lutefisk to Minnesota than it eats itself. A few years ago, a young teenager from Norway visited our family. When offered a heaping plate of the white, gelatinous substance drizzled in butter, he declined. "Only impoverished Norwegians eat lutefisk!" but of course, the impoverished are precisely the people who brought it here in the first place.

Hermoine recalls the annual dinner. "We'd have a big barrel of fish. In cold water. I suppose what they did was get the fish frozen and then thaw it out." Lutefisk dinners occurred in late fall or early winter when temperatures routinely dipped below freezing. No doubt the barrels were stored outside to be kept cold. "The older ladies who did all the cooking, their shoulders would ache—both arms and shoulders all the way up—for a week afterward, because they'd reach into this ice cold water and pull out that fish. Then they'd cook it in great big kettles, so big we don't use them anymore." Modern lutefisk (*lute* means lye) preparation is considerably simplified. All the soaking has been eliminated along with the lye treatment: just thaw, season, boil, and serve. Not so in the '30s, '40s, and '50s.

Lutefisk might impart its name to the event, but in our minds, *lefse* was the centerpiece. It remains today as the most highly work-intensive part. Our own mother, Agnes, made fantastic lefse, a tradition carried on by both daughters and granddaughters, although not all of us have attained her skill level. We always ate it at holiday meals. Ann and I loved the days leading up to a church lutefisk supper because Mom would bake literally thousands of pieces, and the family got to eat the ones that didn't turn out quite perfectly shaped. To make lefse you put boiled potatoes through a ricer, add butter and salt to season, and mix in enough flour to make a soft dough. Using a special grooved rolling pin, you roll out the dough very,

very, *very* thinly into a perfectly round crepe. With a *spurtel* (wooden spatula), you transfer the crepe to a hot lefse iron (griddle) and bake until brown spots emerge. You flip, and bake the opposite side. The finished lefse is folded and stacked between dish towels to keep it moist as it cools. Lefse is eaten according to the style of the area from where its baker's family immigrated. Traditionally it's rolled into a cylinder after being spread with butter; then some families add jams, others sugar, either white or brown. Some even use it as a vehicle for leftover meats and cheeses.

The recipe is simple; the process is not. Ricing a hundred pounds of boiled potatoes, then rolling thousands of rounds from the dough requires muscle. Until it's baked, the dough tears easily. Overbaking causes brittleness; underbaking causes doughiness. Today's lefse grills are electric; the grills Hermoine and Vi remember were heated directly on cast iron stoves where the temperature soared. Hours—days—of such intense labor took its toll. Not everyone was up to the task. Sometimes men were recruited to help with ricing, but after that, the women were on their own. No doubt lefse provided a time of fun and fellowship for the women working together, but muscles would be sore for days afterward.

Serving a meal the magnitude of the lutefisk supper required full participation of the entire congregation, but the Ladies were responsible for the greater share. Women planned, organized, and prepared the food; men and children were recruited for serving. Ellen recalls being recruited at Lime Creek as a young girl of ten or eleven to help with serving. "There was this woman who was always in charge of training the serving girls. She volunteered for the job because she thought she knew more about the proper way to do things than most." At this point in the story, Ellen pauses, not sure of whether or not to go on—she knows full well that the woman in question is one of Ann's and my relatives. "And we girls, well, we thought she was a little bit difficult to please." We sisters exchange an amused glance, remembering fully.

While the ultimate purpose of a lutefisk supper was to earn money (oftentimes enough money to fuel mission projects and local expenses for the whole year), the byproducts were preservation of heritage, congregational and community fellowship, and entertainment. It was—and still is—an evening when folks of Nordic descent celebrate their culture. As the evening progresses, folks' language becomes thicker and thicker with the regional brogue. Memories from earlier days are shared and tales get taller and taller. It takes little effort for us to imagine our own Uncle Buell pushing back from the table, patting his full belly, and declaring, "Ja, den! Dat vas a goot meal!" No one leaves without bestowing *"Takk skal du har"* (thank you) and *"Mange tusen takk"* (many thousand thanks) on cooks and servers.

CHICKEN, HAM AND BEANS, AND SHEETCAKE

Various Ladies Aids sponsored lots of other food events too. The women of Bethlehem Lutheran served chicken dinners on a regular basis throughout the '30s and '40s when small towns in the Midwest, like everywhere else, experienced the nation's economic hardships. The mission statement of Bethlehem's Aid began, "The purpose of this organization shall be as set forth below: to promote and stimulate love for the great mission of the Church." The chicken dinner was the vehicle by which this was directly applied to the surrounding community. It was customary when Aid held its monthly meetings to prepare and serve a full meal. No doubt the practice developed out of earlier days when gathering for a meeting meant giving up the better part of a day by the time horse-drawn transportation was factored in. Since the food had to be prepared anyway, it was no more difficult to make more and share with the community. At Bethlehem, it was usually teachers who came for the meal. In other communities it was equally typical to attract Karl the mechanic or Orvil the post master. At twenty-five cents, the meal was a bargain. In the process, Karl, Orvil, and the teachers saw the "great mission of the Church" in action (Article II, 1.).

The Memorial Day Ham Dinner has been served yearly by the Trinity Ladies Aid/ALCW/WELCA for almost eighty years. The menu is unchanged from the '30s: ham, scalloped potatoes, green beans, salad, and pie. Proceeds go to the cemetery fund. Vi remembers that some members of the congregation once entertained a discussion to allocate the proceeds somewhere else, but "there was a little ruckus, because that money was supposed to go to the cemetery." Even if the dinners were to stop today, the maintenance of Trinity's cemetery is insured for years to come.

Chicken dinners were popular at Trinity as well. Women would bring chickens from their own flocks, and it was assumed that the more unpleasant chores (killing and plucking feathers) would be done at home. Nevertheless, Vi and Hermoine recall at least one time when someone deposited two live chickens at the church. On another occasion an elderly woman who wanted to contribute but wasn't well enough to help with the preparation gave the Ladies a "donation" whose odor betrayed a lack of freshness. Even now they chuckle at the memory. "I guess her sense of smell wasn't too sharp any more, but it stunk! Well, we didn't want to hurt her feelings, so we waited till she wasn't looking, and then a couple of us took it out behind the building and buried it," Hermoine recalls.

It was not unusual for the Ladies Aid to serve dinners off site as well. There were stronger connections between church and community than we can appreciate now. This was especially evident in the two town churches, Emmons and Bethlehem. Emmons had only one church in town, and most of the town's population were members. Buffalo Center had both Catholics and Methodists besides Lutherans, but the presence of several churches only served to strengthen community ties. These were decades when social life centered around church activity, when public schools set aside one afternoon a week for students to receive religious instruction, when all businesses were closed on Sunday, and when no one would schedule a non-church activity on Wednesday evening—"church night"—even outside Advent or Lent. And so the Ladies could often be found cooking meals for the local barn sale, community picnic, public auctions, 4th of July in the park, school events, and the like. An entry in Trinity's Ladies Aid history from 1936 reads, "Lunch served at the corn husking contest at the home of Tom E. Proceeds: $20.26." These events provided a service. It didn't hurt that they also generated monies.

Not every occasion called for a full meal. Ladies Aids were responsible for: One, refreshments after services. (It wasn't only Mom's lefse that was in demand—Sunday morning treats included her blond brownies, maple-snap cookies, and sheetcakes with broiled coconut frosting.) Two, serving "lunch" after funerals. ("Lunch" was the term for anything served beyond coffee but less than a full meal. Lunch could refer to sandwiches, but it also might mean cake and cookies. When you went to someone's home for a visit, you were served lunch then too, and in that case, it probably referred to coffee and homemade donuts.) Three, hostessing bridal and baby showers. (In these cases, a smaller contingency often took charge, usually the circle to which the bride's mother or new grandmother belonged.) Four, feting anniversary couples. ("On October 10, 1936, the Ladies Aid celebrated Mr. and Mrs. John Herfendal's 50th wedding anniversary in the church basement, about 500 people attended," recorded in the history of Trinity's Ladies Aid. *Five hundred!*)

Five, the annual mother-daughter banquet. Mother-Daughter Banquets used to be gala affairs. For a number of sensitive reasons, the modern congregation often nixes them. Blended families where daughters have more than one mother figure, family members divided by great distances, mothers without daughters and daughters without mothers—any and all of these situations are reasons for discomfort around the traditional Mother-Daughter gathering. But in decades past they were all-out affairs, eagerly anticipated. At Emmons, plans were begun far in advance to choose themes, contract speakers, arrange for entertainment, and invite special guests.

Every year the basement social hall was decorated in harmony with the theme for the evening. With enough crepe paper, even the darkest of basements can be transformed into something festive. Special centerpieces (usually doubling as door prizes: "Look under your cup for the special sticker"), table cloths, fancy napkins, and—best of all—*nut cups*. Ann remembers the nut cups as a highlight, the most important element of the evening, probably equally so for Mom as it kept Ann occupied while waiting for things to begin. Nut cups were works of art, lovingly and patiently crafted from paper, intricately folded, taped, and stapled into swans, hats, flowers, or umbrellas. The promise of a nut cup was enough to get even tom-boy Ann willingly into patent leather shoes.

Dinner would be served by the men of the congregation, and they might even have a hand in the final food preparation—but only after weeks of work by the Ladies. For events like this, there were multiple committees: program, decorating, food, door prizes, serving, and cleanup, at the very least. At the last minute, after a complete briefing on how to handle each of the food items, serving would be turned over to the men. I remember one evening when Mom spent as much time running back and forth to the kitchen as sitting at the table. Agnes was on the food committee that year, and she decided it would be festive to serve mixed vegetables in *timbale* (deep-fried batter "baskets") with a white cream sauce dribbled across the top—much, much too complicated for a bunch of men to handle.

Due to the eighteen-year difference in our ages, we two sisters attended a combined total of twenty-two banquets with our mother and grandmother. That's a lot of door prizes ("Who came the farthest?" "Who has the most grandchildren?" "Who has the most buttons on her outfit?") and nut cups.

One of Emmons Ladies Aid's most celebrated events was the Birthday Party. It was such a big deal that our mother would try to get the day off work. I remember Grandma taking me out of school for the afternoon to attend. Even a few men would come. The big attraction was the cakes. Each circle was assigned a month (or two, depending on how many circles there were and the number of members in each circle). The assignment was to decorate the table and a coordinating cake for the month. Competition was fierce. Some months were definitely better than others. If there was a holiday or two, the cakes for those months could be pretty spectacular. December, for instance—you can imagine red poinsettias or stockings with presents or Santa flying across in a sleigh. July was good because of the 4th. February always featured hearts and chocolates. One year September boasted an entire miniature classroom, complete with kids and books. But March—my month—was pretty lean. I always hoped that there were too many people to fit around the table, because then I was allowed to choose a secondary month.

COOKBOOKS

Near the end of the WMF Ladies Aid tenure, the 1950s ushered in the church cookbook phenomenon. If Agnes's maple snaps were popular items on the dessert table, multiply that many times over: *every*body's mother, aunt, and grandmother had a specialty.

Cookbooks became a ministry in and of themselves. The impetus to produce a cookbook came from the same goals outlined in a typical mission statement. Women of the Ladies Aid saw food as ministry. In the dedication page of the Deer Creek Valley Cook Book which lends an epigram to this chapter we read, "To the Homemakers of our church, who are co-workers with God in building strong bodies, and in nurturing immortal souls, this little book is dedicated." Co-workers-with-God-in-the-effort-to-build-strong-bodies-for-their-congregations formed numerous committees to get the job done: collecting recipes from members; soliciting advertising from community sponsors; typing out pages on special mimeograph paper, adding Bible verses to complement each entry; borrowing the church mimeograph machine for printing; and, finally, distributing the finished product.

A typical cookbook took the opportunity to pontificate, if just a little. Under the heading "The necessity of an Adequate Diet," we read,

> A body is the final product of the foods fed to it all the days of its life. Eating wrong foods, or eating to excess, will slow a body and dull a mind before a person has reached middle age. A body needs a "balanced diet." It needs fuels, building materials and regulators, all of which are supplied by the foods we eat. To furnish an abundance of fuel foods and neglect building materials and regulators will result in damage to the human machine. On the other hand, building materials and regulators will not compensate for a lack of fuel foods.

Often recipes were included for such things as good mothering, spirituality, virtue, and the like. A recipe for A Happy Home called for:

4 cups love	2 cups loyalty
3 cups forgiveness	1 cup friendship
5 tbsp hope	2 tbsp tenderness, kindness and understanding
4 quarts faith	1 barrel laughter

It came with instructions, to "Mix love and loyalty thoroughly. Add forgiveness and faith. Blend with tenderness, kindness, and understanding. Add friendship and hope. Sprinkle abundantly with laughter. Bake with sunshine. Serve daily with generous helpings." There were usually advice and pithy sayings as well:

"Sin's forbidden fruit always makes for a bad jam."

"Even a fish wouldn't get into trouble if he kept his mouth shut."

"Providence sends food for the birds but does not throw it in the nest."

Also common was the household hint section. "When selecting a chicken at the market a tender fowl has a flexible breast bone." "Bananas, peaches, pineapple or any fruit you wish, pressed through a sieve and added to a plain tapioca will make the old stand by take on a new fascination."

So was a section on soap-making. Soap recipes typically included fat, Lewis Lye, borax, ammonia, and water. A cooked recipe we found added sugar and sal soda. An *uncooked*—good thing!—recipe added gasoline.

Cookbook or not, certain food items became so standard throughout the years that even now, more than a half century later, you'll likely find them on the church menu. These concoctions come in two categories. In the first are things so ubiquitous they never got submitted as a cookbook entry. How to make them and which occasions call for them seems to be included in Lutheran DNA. In this group are items you'd never serve at home. Most popular are the open-faced-Cheez-Whiz-on-round-"party"-loaf, garnished with one green olive slice in its center, and the plain bread and butter sandwich—two slices processed white bread (Wonder or Hostess) spread with butter and cut down the middle, *never* diagonally. A variation of this last, the "funeral sandwich," includes one thin slice of bologna or ham.

In the second group are dishes from the home kitchen, prolifically varied and experimented upon. So omnipresent are the foods and so prolific the variations that they often got their own cookbook categories: Tuna Casserole and Jello Salads.

Recently we sisters had occasion to attend a funeral at Emmons Lutheran. As we left the house, we reminded Ann's daughter Morgan not to wait supper for us as we'd likely be having "lunch" after the service. "Yeah," she said. "A butter-and-ham-sandwich, white cake with white frosting, Kool-Aid, and coffee." You know what we ate.

THE REWARDS OF FOOD MINISTRY

Gradually the old kitchens were updated or replaced altogether. In Emmons, the 1950s closed with the congregation building a new facility with a modern commercial kitchen. Lime Creek Church has closed its doors, the congregation divided among nearby churches, and the building itself moved from its original location to a new foundation (sans basement) at a living history museum. Bethlehem added on an entire wing which includes a modern kitchen. Today Trinity remains in the same location and the same building where it has stood since 1887, though not without change. A cryptic entry in the Ladies Aid minutes during the '40's reads, "Mrs. E. reported on stoves dropped until meet time [sic]." The following month, this was added: "A secret ballot was taken and was decided in favor of buying a stove. Mrs. F.A. reported on gas stove available at school. Not over $10. 33 voted in favor of this 5 nos. Stove committee will complete details. Motion made and seconded that stove committee get hot water heater [sic]."

When Trinity's ancient kitchen was remodeled, Hermoine was a central figure. Before marriage she had taught home economics in high school, "house planning and that sort of thing." In her words, planning the kitchen was a bit of a battle. "There was a dear lady who was president. She stood in the middle of the kitchen when it was torn up and said, 'I think we'll put the stove there, and we should put a counter over here,' and I thought, well, I don't think so. I thought I'd better go home and see what I could do." She went to bed to sleep on it and awoke with the full design in her head. "But then we had a time with the men! 'You don't need anything better than linoleum on the countertop, and you don't need anything better than just plain linoleum floors.' We really argued with the men for quite awhile." In time, the women prevailed: there's no linoleum on the countertops.

In spite of better, more modern facilities, food preparation—be it for a dozen women gathered for a luncheon meeting or 500 attendees at a lutefisk supper—is hard work. There are generous returns: fun, fellowship, money, and the intrinsic reward of ministry. Before the returns, ministry costs a great deal in the way of time, energy, expertise, and monetary expense. Sometimes, in Ann's and my lifetime, when the number of women working outside the home at full time jobs makes it increasingly difficult to find people to serve at church dinners, we forget that "women's work" within the church has *always* meant hard work and sacrifice. As early as May, 1936, the cost was hinted at in this entry in Trinity's Ladies Aid history: "It was decided that two ladies serve lunch each time instead of only the one." Maybe the expense of ingredients was too high for one person; no doubt finding the time for preparation was difficult; undoubtedly sharing the task was more fun. Again in an entry from the same year, we find evidence that not everyone was willing or able to manage the hard work. "Mrs. R. gave $10.00 in lieu of serving." We'd love to have been present for the conversations that preceded these entries!

An entry from 1947 indicates that the challenge of determining expenses and weighing the value of hard work was ongoing. "It was voted on and carried that 25 cents be charged for afternoon and noon lunches, and that members not serving pay $10.00 instead of $5.00." We assume the money amounts referred to are yearly dues to the organization, though we don't know for sure. At any rate, the entry shows the importance members placed on the value of food service.

Finally, in 1953, we find an indication that at least some people in the Ladies Aid had tired of the constant struggle of serving when "it was voted that each member donate $5.00 instead of a supper." The reference is to the elimination of one specific supper, not church suppers as a whole.

Serving good food was—and is—intimately linked with "promot[ing] and stimulat[ing] love for the great mission of the Church." The vitality of a congregation, and perhaps the church at large, can be credited to a certain extent with the culinary offerings of the Ladies who worked to nourish both bodies and souls through their efforts. Food is ministry, an idea that this cookbook introduction captures:

> Cook books and aprons and dirty dishes can mean only sweat and toil and aching feet. It is the hope and prayer of the ladies of DCV that this assembly of recipes will in some way be useful not only in helping prepare more tasty dishes but that you may also find joy in preparing these

recipes knowing that God giveth food for both body and soul and you are His cook, providing deliciously prepared food for the family He has entrusted to you. Then even a cook book can mean more than aprons and dirty dishes...even a cook book can be an instrument used to the glory of God as you toil in your kitchen...then even a cook book can provide food for both body and soul.

—the Parsonage Family

(From the 1955 cookbook of the Deer Creek Valley Lutheran Church in Northwood, IA; Harvey Gilbertson, Pastor)

Even with the present resurgence of home cooking, few of today's women would call their cookbooks "instruments to the glory of God," nor would they willingly claim "sweat, toil, and aching feet" as strictly female territory. And they shouldn't. Times have changed for the better. Equal rights, equity in career choice, the necessity—and desire—for women to participate in the paid work force, to have careers, to be more than servants, to be appreciated, to make a difference, all these are worthy changes. At the same time, as we move on we can't get so lost in our assertion of rights that we forget how we got here. The Ladies toiled, laughed, cried, and celebrated to work toward a greater cause. The cause: service to people within the congregation, service to community and the world at large, and service to the future—we, their daughters. Food preparation was the vehicle of those efforts. A civilization's identity is as much in its food as in its language or other customs. Yes, the identity is Norwegian, but even more so, the identity is Lutheran: plain, basic, appealing to everyone, not highly spiced or seasoned (except with sweetness), self-effacing, and modest. Feeding people was and continues to be a central way in which the gospel is spread. That's what the Ladies Aid was about.

CHAPTER FIVE
CRAFTS, THE SPIRITUAL GLUE

"Where language falls mute, where reason has produced its
last halting step toward truth, the arts begin..."
—Rev. Dr. Howard E. Friend, Jr.

CRAFTING AND ORGANIZING

All the Ladies were adept at handwork. Alma, Marita, and Linnea took for granted their competence at sewing, knitting, and crocheting. They'd grown up in homes where clothing, draperies, household accessories, bedding, even dish towels were produced on site and where patterns and ideas were passed freely from friend to sister to neighbor. There were no craft stores as we know—no Joanne's or A. C. Moores or Hobby Lobbys. But *The Ladies Home Companion* arrived at some homes. Dry goods stores in Emmons and Buffalo Center carried McCalls and Simplicity patterns, yarn, embroidery floss, and some fabrics. Other fabrics could be mail-ordered through J.C. Penney and Sears. And animal feed and flour really, truly did arrive in printed fabric bags intended for sewing into clothing and towels. Girls were expected to learn to sew. By the time they were ready for marriage, Alma, Marita, and Linnea each had a hope chest filled with crocheted dish cloths, kitchen towels, and hand-embroidered bed linens. They had all learned the basics of handwork, but a few showed special ability, like Marita. Or like Gwen at Trinity and Esther at Bethlehem.

Ann and I read in the written history of the Lime Creek Ladies Aid, "The first record of organized ladies work in Lime Creek congregation was a sale of made articles in 1885."

We listened as Gwen remembered the celebration of her mother's 90th birthday. "We had a mother-daughter tea. Somewhere in a drawer, if I can find it, is a crocheted butterfly. I'll find it one of these days. That was how they honored her at the mother-daughter tea, with a hand crocheted butterfly."

We listened as Esther admitted, "I can't quilt anymore, and it pains me some. Quilting was life. I miss it dreadfully."

Producing "made articles" has always been a large part of Ladies Aid activity. Handwork was definitely a reason to come together—in some cases, the impetus behind organization. The Lime Creek history continues:

> The first record of organized ladies work in Lime Creek congregation was a sale of made articles in 1885. The ladies of pioneer days reported having two sales for the purpose of raising money to pay for furnishing the church for dedication in 1885. One of these sales was held in the road outside of the church and the other was held in the Helge Emmons grove. One article, a candlewick bedspread made by Caroline and Pauline Peterson, was sold at one of these sales. It was purchased for $2.00 by Iver Saue. It had the inscription, '*Foraering til Missionen 1881*,' worked on it in candlewicking. [Translation: For the Purpose of Missions]

We see from the very beginnings that handcrafts were a vehicle of organization, a means to get the neighborhood women to come together. "Sewing was a way for us to have a place and a time to come together," Gwen said. By the 1930s, general Ladies Aid meetings themselves were not normally used for doing handcrafts. Although the records from all four congregations show that sewing and other crafts were a principal way for the Ladies Aids to make money, there was no mention of those activities being done during meetings. Nor in that long listing of offices was there such a thing as Secretary of Handcrafts/Quilting/Sewing. How were such things organized? We read in their reports about funds earned from handcrafts, but there was almost no mention of *how*. Finally Gwen explained (not without a lot of patience on her part). "Everyone knew what she was good at doing, so she usually gravitated toward that circle." No chairwoman was necessary; instead there was an entire structure: the circle.

By 1930, Ladies Aids used the meeting structure and program suggestions provided by the WMF. Unless the program covered a specific craft, there was no formal time for such activity. While there were minutes from general Aid meetings in all the Boxes, only sporadic mention was made about circle activities, usually in a short yearly statement tacked onto the end of the formal Ladies Aid report. Circle members were too busy doing what they'd come to do to waste time on business meetings. With the exception of careful accounting of money raised from various craft projects, we have to rely on verbal accounts.

Many circles were organized by specific crafts. Others became associated with one craft or another as women cycled in and out of membership. By 1945 Bethlehem had seven circles, and four of them were listed in the yearly report by interest topics: Rebecca (needlework), Eunice ("cut carpet rags"), Pheobe (card sales), and Grace (rug-makers). By year's end, Pheobe had earned $77.00 from its card sales, and Eunice $100.55 from rug making. In addition to these four, Esther was listed as focusing on "missions," and Faith-Hope-Charity on "higher education." Martha was the only one without a designated interest. Proceeds all went to missions.

Gwen had been an active member of the Trinity chapter of Lutheran Daughters of the Reformation—the LDR Girls—until she was married. "We went to members' homes, and we embroidered dresser scarves and sold them at the Aid bazaar." Did the LDR Girls take roll? Have dues?

Were there regular business meetings and programs as in the Ladies Aid? "I remember we just embroidered," said Gwen. Young girls were taught to embroider. By age twelve a girl most likely knew all the basics: the running stitch, the lazy daisy, the French knot, and satin stitch. Gwen remembers that girls at Trinity joined the LDR specifically to learn and perfect embroidery stitches. "Our meetings were devotions and embroidery. Maybe ten minutes of devotions and ninety minutes of embroidery." Once they were married—and sufficiently proficient in embroidery?—they transferred over to the Ladies Aid. The LDR Girls was a sort of pre-Ladies Aid, providing younger women with religious training, and evidently someone at Trinity thought unmarried girls needed needlework training as well. It's interesting to note that whenever the subject of the LDR came up, no matter which congregation, they were remembered singularly for embroidery.

Whether circle or LDR members, the Ladies saw themselves as workers. In many ways, membership in the circle was more important than in the Ladies Aid itself. Perhaps it felt more real. As Hermoine had told us when we talked about organization, "People at the synod or district level could haggle about whatever they haggled about—theology, procedures, rules, doctrine—we were mostly just concerned about getting the work done." It was good to be of use. Time could be justified when a product was realized. Circles got the work done.

With handcrafts, product and process were equally revered. To give a handmade gift was the highest kind of benevolence. To make something beautiful was to engage in one of life's richest experiences. After food preparation, handcrafts are the most important social activity of our groups. Women's handwork was often responsible for the trappings that made a congregation function as a faith-based group with faith-based (both holy and mundane) symbols. Churches needed paraments, choir robes, and pastoral robes; they also needed curtains, banners, Christmas costumes, dish towels, infant layettes, baptismal cloths, and the like. Most of these were produced by hand.

Crafts made a lot of money. Together with earnings from lutefisk suppers, dues and various offerings, the proceeds from the selling of handcrafted products rounded out yearly budgets. Without the women's handiwork, there wouldn't have been benevolences for missions or kitchen supplies or hymnals in the pews or all of the other things that satisfy the soul and make a church run smoothly. Whenever the Ways and Means chairwoman and her committee were responsible for finding ways of making money, they relied most often on craft sales.

These two forces—spiritual satisfaction and capital procurement— made crafting important and enduring to our Ladies.

CRAFTING AND SPIRITUALITY

Our contemporary friend Margareta, a dedicated and talented designer, says it best. "To make something pretty is to worship. Creating is godlike; it's when we're closest to God. To do it together is to worship in community. When words fail, the *act* of creating suffices." As we think about Margareta's definition, we think about the words *creator* and *creation*. The Ladies were engaged in "making pretty things" through being creative. They would not, however, have readily admitted to being *creators* or that their works were *creations*. "Only God creates," Hermoine reminded us. "People just make things." While we readily agree, we also find several parallels between the Creator and these "makers of pretty things."

An artist or craftswoman is said to be *inspired*, literally, "breathing in the Spirit" [Greek]. What is produced through inspiration, then, might be holy, an expression of the soul. Michelangelo said art is "a shadow of the divine perfection." The Ladies might not have been consciously thinking about Michelangelo's words, but surely as they played with design and color to "make pretty things," their thoughts soared above the mundane, at least for a few hours.

"We humans are creative beings by nature," says Alma. "Without creativity, life goes nowhere."

"Yes," adds Marita; "and creating something of beauty feels like prayer." Creativity, then, becomes a form of worship. It takes the mind to a place of prayer, of meditation, of intention, a phenomenon especially true in repetition of a physical action. Buddhists would call it Zen; or Taoists, Wu Wei; or the Chinese, Feng Shui, but the Ladies called it prayer. Creativity in community builds fellowship, an important part of Lutheran faith. Lutherans believe that fellowship—whether in the holiness of a worship service or in more social gatherings—is central.

Creativity is also communication. Again, we think of Margaret's words. "When words fail, the act of creating suffices." To speak of serious things is difficult. For the Ladies, shared handwork was communication when words failed. Activities done in community grease the gears of conversation. Tough subjects, private subjects, even holy subjects are easier to articulate when the activity requires concentration and eyes don't have to meet. Because the Ladies were do-ers, emotions that could not be easily talked about or could not be explained found expression in doing.

Nobody knew this better than Alma, Marita, and Linnea. "There's a stereotype about us Norwegians, you know, but stereotypes usually come from degrees of reality."

"We're taught to talk when we have something to say. Other ethnic groups talk in order to find something to say."

"To speak of serious things—ideas of the soul, beliefs about art or life or God—is difficult. Sometimes the right words don't come; sometimes the words we have feel embarrassingly revealing." Marita put this in practical terms for us. "Around a quilt frame, even the quiet ones get to participate. You don't have to say a word to know you're still part of the group."

"It was evangelization too," says Linnea. Knowing that the product of their hands was destined to warm someone or minister to someone was what the Ladies were all about. In truth, few were wealthy in the ways that

America has always defined wealth, however, they knew they enjoyed blessings that were hard to come by elsewhere: the guarantee of daily food, a roof over their heads, medical treatment when they needed it. More importantly, they felt blessed spiritually, and that knowledge needed to be shared. When a finished quilt was sent to Lutheran World Relief, it went with a prayer to minister to spiritual as well as physical need. Prayerfully embroidered pillowcases might bless someone's sleep. Plain hats and mittens would keep a child warm, but brightly colored hand-knitted ones would cheer them as well. No matter what the craft, someone was sure to benefit.

"What could we do about someone in the inner city without a home? Well, we couldn't solve her problems, but we could make something to keep her warm."

"What could we do for people in the mission field? Maybe having something pretty helped them through when they were having a bad day."

"Or on the reservation? We sewed little girls' dresses one year to send to our Indians in the Dakotas."

"We could minister through our handwork."

"To create something of beauty and then to give it away is to worship twice."

"All this talk about creativity is true, but let's be frank," says Marita. "Making stuff is just plain fun!" When you're having fun, you're present only in the activity at hand and not worrying about everything else. It's healthy escapism, and there was plenty for the Ladies to escape from: the Great Depression (jobs, food, housing, clothing, health) and the War (injuries, death). "In the end, after all the high-falutin' words, we do it for fun."

Esther knew what she was talking about: Quilting *is* life. In our last conversation together, she bragged a little about her quilting. "Everyone was always amazed at how I could use my fingernail to push the needle through, not a thimble. Everyone was always amazed at that ability!" She eschewed the use of a thimble because she wanted to *feel*. Her creative experience was total physical participation, total immersion.

Esther was a physical person. In the days when girls and women weren't encouraged to do sports, her favorite things were playing ball with her children and going fishing. "Oh, I loved to fish! Bullheads were my favorite! I'd catch 'em by the dozens. Then I always did my own scaling and cleaning. I'd fry 'em up for the family."

In time she became too old to play ball or go fishing, and then quilting became even more important. Esther directed the quilting group at church. When at last she had to give up quilting, partly because of failing eyesight, partly because being tethered to oxygen made everything more difficult, life narrowed. "Well, I had to give up baseball a long time ago, and there's no kids around the house now anyways. It hurt too when I couldn't fish any more. But quilting—I miss it dreadfully."

CRAFTING AND EVANGELIZING

Further on in the Lime Creek History we get an idea of other sorts of handicrafts the women worked on. Among their projects were "church seats" (padding or pillows?) and sewing "hickory sorter" (a striped material used for men's shirts). There were nearly as many forms of creative expression as there were Ladies Aid members. While embroidery enjoyed longevity, some other crafts were more obscure and fell by the wayside rather quickly after their zenith. Gwen remembers the "quilling" phase in the '40s: "The best held demonstrations to teach the rest of us. One year the whole bazaar was practically quilling. Greeting cards, tiny pictures to be hung on the wall, small jewelry boxes—beyond that, what could you do with it that would last? What was practical? Too frivolous, too impractical." There were other crafts that suffered the same fate: decoupage, smocking, papier mache, bottlecap wreathes, tin punching....the list goes on and on. Some crafts, though not always well known, stayed in vogue because they harked back to the Old Country. Hardanger embroidery, black-and-white embroidery work, and rosemaling are some examples.

While crafting organized the Ladies into circles, crafting also served to bring smaller groups into the whole. Occasionally a circle would present a how-to session for a regular Aid meeting. Invitations would be sent out to unchurched friends and announcements placed in the local paper. In this way, a popular craft served as a tool for evangelism.

By far the largest evangelism-through-crafts effort was the annual bazaar. "Crafts gave us a time and place to come together. We did a lot of that. Little by little it got to be a bazaar," reports Gwen. The idea of the bazaar need time to develop. A story is told in their history about earlier Ladies of Trinity:

> When the ladies had been working for a year and a half with their sewing they had made many useful garments together with two very pretty quilts. They decided to sell numbers on these quilts. They were getting along splendidly with their numbers and were quite proud of their success, but their rejoicing changed when Rev. Christenson told them that he did not approve of their method in getting money. The ladies were perfectly innocent and very sorry for the wrong they were doing and suggested they return the money to each individual that had purchased a number. This he did not want them to do but he did want them to promise, "Never again to use a method of this kind to produce money." And that promise has been kept in the Ladies Aid to this day.

The annual bazaar was the solution to money-making without direct solicitation or the selling of numbers. Every Lady we interviewed talked about the bazaar as a highlight of the year. Often it was held pre-Christmas for the simple reason that Christmas outdid and outshone every other season. At any given bazaar, even if not held in the traditional fall time-frame, well over half of the items held Christmas themes. Christmas outshines all other holidays for decorating potential. Easter, Valentines, July 4th, Halloween, and Thanksgiving all pale in comparison. Christmas was the holiday that gave everyone permission to decorate—and anything went. Wreaths and ornaments were fashioned from almost any material, from fabric to yarn to clothespins to bottle caps. No matter how contrived or tacky the item, it would sell. Everyone could be counted on to purchase something of the latest craze and exhibit it with pride. "The mayor's wife, the banker's wife—they might have homes furnished with furniture and accessories from expensive stores," said Gwen, "but come Christmas they all hung bottle-cap wreaths on the front door."

The Christmas Bazaar was the annual money bonanza. Often held at night, more often than not, the men attended as well. Our friend Bev from Trinity, a long-time bazaar participant, joined in the discussion. "The men would bid more than the women; they'd really get into it. I remember my husband and another man would bid each other up every year till the amounts got so high they really couldn't afford it, and they'd act like they were angry, but they were really good friends. Oh, they had a ball." Ann and I suggest that perhaps an advantage to having the men there was that they were more competitive, hence, bidding each other up. "Competitive! Ha!" Gwen interrupts with a chuckle. "Ann knows what happens when I bid!" Bev stepped in again. "Ah, but she's right. The men always went higher! Ole Christianson used to be the auctioneer, before we got Roy. And the men would come, and they would bid really well on quilts and things, you know? Even back in the '40s those quilts would go for a hundred dollars or more. *Because the men did the bidding!* But then when the men quit coming, we didn't make so much."

Trinity's nighttime bazaar was typical. Bev explains, "Everything that the women made was displayed on the west half of the basement," and the east half was set with tables for food and chairs for the auction. Big room dividers (portable chalkboards or folding screens) were used to display large items like quilts. Dish towels and pillowcases were pinned and hung together in sets. There were clothes and doll clothes, knitted hats and mittens, puppets, flower arrangements (real and artificial), aprons (an industry in itself), fabric painting (especially with tube paints, a substitute for embroidery for those who never perfected that skill), crochet, basketry, wood-working and metal-working, decorated coffee cans, tooled cans, quilled cans (beer can dollhouse furniture was most popular), tatting, cake decorating, crewel, paint-by-number, appliqué, wooden birdhouses, plaster molding, spool knitting and spool toys, applehead or walnuthead dolls, cornhusk dolls, clothespin dolls, fabric dolls, pipe cleaner art, pinecone and seed art, crocheted granny squares, macaroni pictures, macramé, needlepoint, and crocheted clothes hangers! Bev remembers one woman in particular—Clare—who used to spend the whole year knitting slippers with little pompoms, forty or more pairs. The auctioneer would hold them up, the high bidder would get first choice, and the others interested could choose in order.

Usually a bake sale accompanied the bazaar, and after, a cake walk or a box social. A cake walk was like musical chairs with numbers one through fifteen or however many cakes had been donated. There was always a riotous contest for the fanciest cake, and competition for the best would be both vigorous and silly. "The men were best for that!" remembers Gwen. A variation was the cookie walk.

Box socials provided money and a bit of romance too. Traditionally, teenaged girls and unmarried women—often the LDR Girls—made and packed a lunch in a cardboard box or basket, then decorated it. The boxes were auctioned to teenaged boys and single men, and the lunch inside was shared between cook and high bidder. Supposedly each box was anonymous, and, supposedly, what was inside it had been prepared by the owner herself and not her mother.

Earnings from such an evening of fun were substantial. At Trinity, the 1934 bazaar netted $45.59, and the figure rose steadily over the next few years as people emerged from the Depression: $68.36 in 1935 to $83.28 in 1936 to $129.25 in 1938. By 1942 earnings were up to $221.55 from handcrafts and another $106.73 from food.

THE QUEEN OF CRAFTS: QUILTING

"Reading our quilt is like reading the history of Trinity," says Bev. Ann and I stand with her in front of two quilts hanging on the east wall of Trinity's basement fellowship hall. One is from the 1930s and boasts the names of each of the Trinity founding families. The other is big; *really* big. It's a classic friendship quilt. Made in 1937, each individual block bears the embroidered name of a Trinity family.

To understand what it means to Trinity, Ann and I have to get over all the ideas we've layered onto quilting in recent years. We enjoy it as an industry of pleasure, but a very capitalist one. Modern quilting is complicated. Our needs are many: rotary cutters, self-healing cutting mats, rulers in a variety of shapes and sizes, pattern books, templates, special threads, tapes, and a host of other accoutrements. We can't begin a quilt without a trip to a special quilt fabric store, preferably one that orders from specialized quilt fabric manufacturers. Once we've collected all the equipment and managed to cut and piece together a quilt top on our special Patchwork Edition sewing machines, we either mount it on an expensive wooden frame specially designed for hand quilting, or we send it out to be machine quilted by a professional. For us, the craft of quilting is a stab at artistic expression in a world in which we're continually influenced by people hired to tell us what we want or need. Everything we buy is planned out by interior designers, produced in factories, and sold to us through professional advertising. Even what we make by hand is produced from things manufactured and packaged for our consumption by marketing experts.

The Ladies quilted without such baggage. They used recycled fabrics. Equipment consisted of a pair of scissors, a good ruler, pins, and needles. Piecing designs were derived from known folk patterns handed down from earlier generations. Much of the piecing was done by hand, although some forward-looking women, like our Grandma Clara, used a treadle Singer machine. Once pieced, the top was stretched for hand quilting on a frame put together by someone's husband from two-by-fours. The Ladies' reasons for quilting were for fellowship and friendship and—most importantly—for charity: *Foraering til Missionen.*

Today Ann belongs to a quilting club that meets once a month. Other than the meeting place itself—a church fellowship hall—very little overlays with the Ladies' quilting sessions. Ann's club begins its gathering with an actual business meeting. This is followed by a demonstration or lesson, a group activity (a fabric-swapping game, for instance), then refreshments and announcements. Included in the announcements are upcoming quilt shows and contests, buying trips, news about local fabric stores that stock the hottest fabrics, and directions for participating in a block-of-the-month event. Modern quilting is an industry.

A generation ago, the Ladies met differently. The quilt frame was a permanent fixture in the church basement. The quilts our Ladies Aid made weren't of Biblical traditions like African American story quilting, nor were they like earlier faith quilts that spawned "Christian" piecing patterns ("Cross in the Square," "Star of Bethlehem," "Robbing Peter to Pay Paul"). They were less obvious, less self-conscious about connections to faith.

Of course, Alma, Marita, and Linnea were quilters. "We made one where we embroidered signatures from everyone in the congregation, men, children, *everyone.*"

"One lady spilled coffee on a quilt still on the frame. Of course it couldn't be cleaned, so we just splashed coffee all over it! And it came out looking antique. It was our favorite!"

"Some folks don't have any idea how to store a quilt. The best way is flat on a bed. If you can't do that, put it in a cotton pillowcase. *Never* let plastic touch it!"

Quilts were the royal moneymakers. By 1950, at an auction, a single quilt could bring in more than $100. Esther told us how a half dozen of the Bethlehem Ladies organized in the '50s to finish quilt tops. Finishing meant taking the top design which someone had already pieced or embroidered, layer it with batting in the middle to a backing of more fabric, then hand stitch the whole thing together and finish the edges. "After they were sewn, we stored them in the attic, and once, one was stolen. I won't tell you who it was, but we had our suspicions. Imagine—she had to go through three doors to get to it!" Esther's group charged $60.00 apiece to finish, then sent them off to every state in the union, "including Alaska and Hawaii even before they were states!" According to Esther, all told, between $3,500 and $4,000 was earned and sent off to missions through their little business!

A chief objective of quiltmaking was to send donations through the district to Lutheran welfare organizations. Lutheran World Relief, which had operated since 1945, was the largest and most familiar. All of our congregations participated steadily throughout the WMF decades. Ann and I clearly remember Grandma Clara and our mom Agnes talking enthusiastically about quilting for Lutheran World Relief. Fabric leftover from making our own clothes ended up there, as did some of our outgrown skirts and blouses. We took it for granted that our castoffs would be reinvented and sent off to Asia and Africa. As a child I had a Little Golden Book with a picture of an African mother in a tree house wrapping a quilt around her small child. I could easily imagine my own dresses superimposed on the page.

Quilting accomplished objectives closer to home too. Records from all four congregations list gift quilts for new babies, for retiring pastors, to honor anniversaries, to thank someone for a job well done, or to comfort someone in illness or grief. Ann has one of those quilts in her possession. It's delicate lilac on white and features flowers with meticulously appliquéd petals. One hundred sixty names are embroidered on it, and both men and women are represented in the signatures. Divergent stitching styles show that there were multiple embroiderers and multiple stitchers. Close examination reveals what appear to be coffee stains, or perhaps blood. Friction spots hint at continual use. One can imagine it draped around invalid shoulders. According to the story Ann was told, it was made by friends to comfort a woman suffering from "lingering disease" (probably tuberculosis). To look at this quilt is to realize the lives of many people coming together and caring for one another and to think about living, loving, celebrating, and suffering.

After the recipient died, the quilt lay in an attic until a family member discovered it and decided Ann should be entrusted with its care.

Properly, Ann stores it in a cotton pillowcase.

CHAPTER SIX
"A DAILY GIFT—A DAILY PRAYER"
MISSION BOXES AND PENNY-A-MEALS

That all societies in the WMF send at once as large a sum of money as possible to H. O. Shurson's office for the National Lutheran Council to be used for spiritual work among the men and women who are in the service of our country.

-Fort Dodge Circuit Missions report for 1948

THE FINER PORTION

When it came to mission work, the Aid needed the combined talents of all the Almas, Maritas, and Linneas.

Linnea remembers, "You know it was sort of exciting the day we handed out those little paper banks to all the Ladies. Shaped like teepees, they were."

"Oh, we cut and glued for hours to get those ready," laughs Marita.

"Maybe teepees wouldn't be politically correct these days, but they were appropriate back in those years—what better symbol for a money collection for the Indian school?" says Alma. "Those teepees could be placed on kitchen tables or window sills or on end tables and they'd keep reminding us about the school and our little girl who went there. What was her name? Doreen? Darlene? Something like that."

"No different, really, than people adopting a child these days to send money to Guatemala or Indonesia."

"We served a luncheon of what we thought were Indian-like foods the day we collected them—corn, rice, beans."

Each year the Aids of Emmons, Lime Creek, Bethlehem, and Trinity Lutheran collected dues, accumulated dinner proceeds, and netted craft sale profits. Once a year the Penny-a-Meal Box—a small cardboard box that sat on each member's kitchen table or window sill—was brought to Aid to be counted. After expenses were met, some monies went back to the congregation for capital projects or general maintenance, but a good portion—if not the greater portion in numbers, always the *finer* portion— was donated to mission work. The Ladies Aid cared deeply about the needs of the world, both locally and globally.

Women of the Evangelical Lutheran Church, through their Women's Missionary Federation, had a long history of mission support. Founda- tions for mission work had been laid in the prior century when, as early as 1837, women in Cobleskill, NY, formed an educational fund to train missionaries. Ruth Fritz Meyer writes in *Women on a Mission* that a group of pastors' wives meeting in a home one afternoon decided by unanimous approval to pledge both money and encouragement toward the education of prospective missionary Walter Gunn (36). Twenty-five years later, closer to home and synod, women in Decorah, IA, organized a "sewing circle" whose function was to "sew and sell articles to the stores to help pay the debt on the new college there" (Luther College). So by the time our Ladies Aids were formed, there was already a rich tradition of mission work.

"Mission work" encompassed a lot. Any number of projects could be construed to fall under its umbrella. In general, it was any effort or money not used to carry on internal business or maintenance of the local facility. After that, the lines blurred. Outgo was complex. Mission work certainly included contributions towards the salary of a foreign missionary or the purchase of education materials to use in mission effort, but what about contributions toward the local parish pastor's salary? Missions encompassed gifts—both monetary and practical—to orphanages, homes for unwed mothers, and Indian schools, but not necessarily books bought for the town or local school library, even when those materials were thematically evangelical. Money sent to the Red Cross or Seamen's Mission was definitely mission, but money collected for area Bible camps might be placed in another category. And then there was the sometimes sticky problem of money sent to and through the circuit, district, or synod. Such contributions were liable to misgiving: where did they go, how much was used for actual mission as opposed to costs, and why were individual congregations obligated to participate? Perhaps one of the appeals of quilting for Lutheran World Relief was that local congregations could be assured no part was taken for operational costs, and the visual object was assurance to donors of its eventual use.

Although the Ladies were always eager to talk about how they raised money (crafts, food), no one wanted to talk about dispersing it...that would have been boasting. As a consequence, Ann and I were obliged to dig very deeply into The Boxes. Our Ladies Aids left both monthly and yearly financial reports. Money amounts were carefully recorded. However, notations for where and how individual amounts were allocated are not always obvious. No doubt both the women who were making out the reports and those who read them had common understanding about how money was spent. Fifty years later, however, details are lost. Since we aren't privy to their conversations, a certain amount of interpretation and reader's license has to be applied. While the same phenomenon is common to any organization or club, it seems more evident in these records, especially in contrast to how carefully names—names of officers, names of committee chairwomen, names of members, names of regional delegates—were noted. We think this speaks to the fact that always—*always*—people and their stories were important; numbers and money amounts were important only in how they supported or reflected people.

The reader will see that the Ladies were extraordinarily generous. They were conscientious in attending to and caring for less fortunate folks. They were aware of their own riches, even during times of personal want. And they were tirelessly fair and accurate, down to the last penny, a fact illustrated in one end-of-the-year financial statement which was amended three separate times—all for the difference between $1.27 and $2.58.

PLACING OURSELVES IN THE WORLD

Missions. Even the word was magic. It conjured up visions of dark places, of intrigue, of mystery. As Ellen recounts, "Hearing visiting missionaries talk about their work in foreign countries was so exciting!" Like most of our women, Ellen had never been outside the United States, and part of the draw of supporting missions and missionaries was to feel as if you were broadening your world horizon, expanding your vision and able to feel a connection to peoples and cultures you knew you would never experience firsthand. A missionary returning from the field would give a talk, show some photos, pass around wooden carvings or fabrics or chopsticks, and a woman whose closest connection to anything outside the borders of the U.S. was an occasional letter from a now-distant cousin in Norway could wonder and imagine. There was the exotic.

There can also be a dark side. When we're honest with ourselves, we admit there's an element of titillation as we vicariously experience the "other." We hear or read about poverty or paganism, and we're thankful we're not "them." It's easy then to feel blessed, and in such a blessed state, it's easy to feel superior. However, as hard as we looked at the written legacies the Ladies left and as closely as we listened to their taped interviews, we could find nothing of arrogance, only benevolence. Perhaps women who are scarcely a generation away from their immigrant roots and who are living through or have just lived through national depression and a world war have little tolerance for pride.

Benevolence brings satisfaction. To know there is something to do to ease another's suffering, to spread the gospel, or to right material inequities is hugely rewarding. Recipient and donor alike reap blessing reflective of the gift. Ellen's visiting missionary provided proof of what their money did.

As Ellen says, "the missionary was on a pedestal." During the '50s, the Emmons congregation supported a specific missionary in Madagascar. To pray for him and his family and to save dimes in a specially designated cardboard box was to feel you were making a difference in the world. This was a man who talked to Africans, sat with them in their crude houses, walked with them over dusty paths, shopped in their open-air markets, taught them, and worshipped with them. He'd learned to speak their language. To Emmons, he was witness to the reality of Africa. "We thought of him as living on a higher plane, even higher than our pastor—after all, he'd given up life in America for the Kingdom."

Records from the ELCA archives (www.elca.org/archives/missionaries) tell that from the '30s to the late '50s, the ELC sent missionaries to two different African nations (Madagascar and South Africa), to five locations in Asia (China, Hong Kong, Taiwan, Japan, and the Cameroons), and to South America (Brazil and Columbia). At any given time, the ratio of congregations to missionaries was large enough to make it unlikely that one would emerge from your local church, but congregations were kept abreast of missionary numbers, locations, and activities through their districts and circuits, and even assigned specific missionaries for prayer support and monetary contributions. A good example is missionary Carola Mosby to Japan. The Archives show Miss Mosby graduating first from the 2-year Waldorf College in Iowa, then attending the Lutheran Bible Institute in Minnesota, and finally graduating with a BA from Augsburg College, also in Minnesota. Mosby served in Japan, beginning as a single woman in 1951, continuing with her missionary husband, Rev. Kenneth Stenberg, until 1957.

The Resolutions set by the St. Ansgar Circuit (Bethlehem's circuit) WMF meeting at Rock Creek Church in Osage, Iowa, in 1951 included, "That we encourage each local aid to contribute annually towards our two circuit projects—namely the scholarship fund and the support of Carola Mosby, our missionary to Japan…" A point later in the same Resolutions asked that the "Chapel in Japan" be a recipient of the meeting's thank offering, after expenses were paid.

By 1951, Bethlehem's Ladies Aid had a history of missionary consciousness. Its constitution, adopted in 1937, was mission-oriented. Articles II.2 and II.3 read, "To disseminate knowledge of missions in general and of the Norwegian Lutheran Church of America in particular" and to "aid financially the missionary activities of the Norwegian Lutheran Church of America through its various mission boards." [Refreshing readers' merger memories: The Norwegian Lutheran Church merged with several others in 1917 to become the Evangelical Lutheran Church, lasting until the 1960 merger into the American Lutheran Church, and finally in 1988 to the Evangelical Lutheran Church in America.]

Emmons' experience felt closer to home. Rev. Kermit Roisen grew up in the Lime Creek Church where he was confirmed as a teenager. Since Lime Creek and Emmons shared the same pastor during these years, Emmons knew him almost as well as Lime Creek. When he began his missionary service in Madagascar in 1953, both congregations supported him as their own. Their close relationship was maintained throughout his tenure in Africa as Roisen corresponded regularly to both communities, even visiting whenever he returned to the States. Such periodic visits did much to keep the missionary field real and close.

Trinity too had its missionary. Their circuit supported the Rev. Lewis Davidson who served in Japan. Like the others listed above, he began his service in the early '50s. The ELC (and former members such as the Norwegian Lutheran Church) had been placing missionaries in Africa a long time, with South Africa's mission field established as early as 1844. By the end of the century, the ELC had sent its first missionaries to Madagascar, then Hong Kong and China. It wouldn't be until sometime after WWII—1949—that Japan would be included. South America also received its first ELC missionaries about the middle of the 20th Century.

Surely being conscious of foreign missions, of individual missionaries, and of the wider church's activity throughout Africa, Asia, and South America was important for placing oneself in the world. Also important was placing oneself into a national context. The needs were great within America, and the Ladies Aid rose to the challenge. The picture of total Ladies Aid support to benevolences outside local congregations during these years is broad and deep. Orphanages, homes for unwed mothers, nursing homes, Indian missions, schools, servicemen (during the War, but not exclusively), colleges, and Bible camps were some. Branching out, there were national organizations such as the Red Cross and the Seamen's Mission, Bible societies, and various homes in places as near as Beliot, Wisconsin, or as far away as Alaska: "If you haven't all ready [sic] done so, won't you this very day, send your 'Dollars for Nome' to your circuit" (Fort Dodge District Gathering Report for '55, p. 8). Giving was not necessarily directed by the Circuit or District or Synod; perhaps donations were instigated by someone within the congregation and then continued on indefinitely once the donation became a line item in the budget, as often happens with church budgets. How could one say no to a worthy cause? Conversely, the women asked themselves, what would a recipient do if expected funds suddenly stopped? How could an organization that had come to rely on donations be turned down?

Some of the difficulties we found in identifying or quantifying financial specifics include arcane references to recipients of foreign mission aid from each congregation. Beneficiaries are listed variously as Lutheran World Relief and Lutheran Welfare, but also as "special missions," "foreign missions," or—as in Trinity's records from 1939—simply "other places in need." Only partial records remain from some years, and other years are missing entirely.

In many cases, apparent donations fall under the heading of "activities" or "service" rather than "mission," and those items get complete disregard as gifts, even though they entailed an outlay of money with no expectation of reimbursement. Bethlehem and Trinity historians left cryptic notes about serving community meals throughout the Depression and war years. Putting these together with reminiscences from our women, we know that church Ladies opened their kitchens sometimes for whole communities to come for a meal, either free or for a small donation. Our friend and community historian Addie recalls that after the Depression, when her Aid group decided to raise the weekly luncheon fee from ten cents to twenty-five cents, some folks complained, even though "it was just ridiculous to argue with twenty-five cents for lunch! Just let them try to make a meal for that!"

Contributions to individuals may or may not have constituted "mission" donations. A 1937 entry in Bethlehem's financial records includes "$25. to Mr. Swenson." There are no other mentions of his name, even in records from the years immediately before and after this entry, and seventy years later there's no way of knowing whether Mr. Swenson was a town merchant, a church janitor, or someone truly in need. Though seemingly isolated, Mr. Swenson is not alone; we found other names scattered similarly throughout.

Part of the problem lies in each individual historian's esoteric record-keeping, but in many cases, time has erased our ability to connect to an organization. Even meticulously detailed treasury accounts list now-obscure recipients such as "mission cottages," "the welfare society," "orphan's home," and "Old Peoples' House." And what was the "Book Mission"? Many recipients are organizations or homes no longer in existence: Emmons records from 1939 list the Ebenezer Home and Lake Park Children's Home, and Bethlehem lists the Aaso Haugen Home, the Story City Home, and the Lutheran Girls' Home, each having been given sizable amounts.

Gifts weren't always cash either. One of our churches records that clothing, bedding, furniture, and canned goods were sent simply to "South Dakota" one depression year. Not only were there non-cash donations, in some cases there wasn't even an identifiable article involved. Goods could be earned by saving Green Stamps and Gold Bond Stamps (both redeemable at company redemption centers for various household and personal items). Product "points" were earned through purchasing items like Butternut Coffee, with the points supposedly transferred over to a worthy organization. Likewise, Betty Crocker points were either redeemed for goods or transferred to an organization.

Perhaps what we do know from their records is more important to seeing the complete picture. We know, for instance, that Bethlehem is repeatedly listed on its circuit honor roll for mission work, once as being the third highest in the circuit for charitable donations. We know that in one year alone, they sent 118 quarts of canned goods to the Good Samaritan Home in Mason City, and that they contributed yearly to the support of an "Indian Girl," Doretta, sending her clothes and spending money month by month for at least five years. We know that Trinity's women canned and sent fifty-seven quarts of fruit to the Beloit Children's Home and collected two boxes of clothing for the Indian Mission at Wiltenbury (both in Wisconsin), and we know that Emmons regularly supported Bethany Indian Missions.

Bethlehem's record from 1932 paints a full picture. That year the Ladies donated $295.50 to charities and paid 43% of the pastor's salary. (His total pastoral salary for '32 was $696.00, a figure considerably higher than the yearly income of most of his parishioners.) Perhaps these figures no longer represent huge pots of money to us today, but adjusting to our own income levels, they translate to a charitable donation of almost $30,000.00! Realize this figure was earned by a group of several dozen women, mostly farm wives with *no* salary of their own.

How It Worked

Dues—varying from ten cents a meeting to a quarter—were collected monthly from each member, and for the most part, that money was intended to be used for operating costs. Other ways were employed to collect for mission work. These can be grouped in at least four categories: box work, special offerings, mission dinners, and collection drives. The first of these required a special chairperson, and it was a sizeable job.

Every Aid elected a Box (or Boxwork) Chair for the year whose job it was to oversee mission collections. Part of the job of the Boxwork chair was to spread the word that "every WMF member has a vital role in evangelism. She can effectively witness for her Lord through her Christ-centered life, and by sharing the story of Jesus with others" (Fort Dodge Report, p 7). The District provided the chair with suggestions and directions about the year's mission program as to where money was to be directed and each Aid's suggested contribution responsibility. Above all, she was to see that the Mission Box motto became reality: "A daily gift—a daily prayer, that all the world my Christ may share." District checkpoints evaluating a successful campaign included:

- Does every member of your Aid have a mission box?
- Did you have a special Mission Box Day and program at the September Aid Meeting when boxes were collected and re-distributed for the coming year?
- Did you have a Home Mission Program in March? Mission boxes, program materials, mission slides and tracts are all available at WMF headquarters (9).

Each Aid was to provide and prominently display their mission box. Whether cardboard or wooden, it appeared at each gathering, at the door, on the speaker's table, at a luncheon table. Contributions were made at member discretion. The Box Chair received materials to be presented at each meeting to encourage members. These were usually short reports highlighting causes. "Every WMF member can have a vital part in the mission work of our church through prayer, daily witnessing, and giving through the Mission Box"(1).

The Mission Box was the largest and most centralized program from the districts. The South Central District, which included Bethlehem Lutheran Ladies Aid, encompassed thirty-six separate Aid groups with a total membership of 4000. Their 1948 mission box receipts totaled $3065.04, equally divided among its mission projects. "Yes, prayers are sorely needed," read its report, "but the Lord also says, 'Give...' and the little Mission Box pleads, 'Use Me.'"

Another box activity was the Penny-a-Meal program. The District provided little printed cardboard collection boxes, one per family, which the Aid distributed throughout the congregation. The idea was to keep the box on the kitchen table and have each family or family member contribute a penny a meal. When the box was full it was brought to the church to be counted. Apparently this was a pretty lucrative method of collection. Emmons Ladies Aid finance accounts for 1939 list $28.08 collected from their mission box and $123.64 from penny-a-meals.

Special offerings came under the chairmanship of another elected office, that of Self Denial. Variously called "thank offerings," "self-denial offerings," or simply "worship offerings," these collections also went toward missions. Boxwork and Self Denial appear in the records as separate jobs with separate responsibilities, the difference being that Self Denial was more devotionally-centered and less directed at specific charities.

The idea of a mission dinner is perhaps self-explanatory. Also in the Emmons records for '39, the Aid collected $46.90 from a special mission dinner, which amount was added to boxwork contributions for a grand total of $198.62. To help put this enormous amount into context, some national figures from the US Bureau of Labor Statistics might be of use: through the later half of the '30s, a typical American family income allowed for an annual savings of $11.00. Imagine increasing what an average family saves in a year nearly twenty times!

A final category included all sorts of collection drives. There were clothing drives, canned goods drives, furniture drives, book drives, drives for school supplies, and drives for toys—whatever the need, it could be met by a drive. Some Aids even have records of appliance drives. Just as they are today, drives were a good way to recycle, hopefully not just to get rid of unwanted articles. Although well-intentioned, it's conceivable that sometimes donations from drives were difficult to regulate. An announcement from the Fort Dodge District gathering report for 1955 reads, "To avoid duplication and other problems, it is advised to contact Dr. Rolf Syrdal, Executive Secretary of the Board of Foreign Missions, before deciding on special projects such as gifts of appliances, clothing, Bibles, etc."

An aside. We're not sure which category the "traveling basket" fits into, but it seems worth mentioning. We found this enigmatic handwritten entry in Bethlehem's 1940 WMF report: "The traveling basket--$7.74 (basket lost so second half was never received)." Sadly, none of the women we interviewed remembered the traveling basket.

Once funds were collected, they needed disbursement. As we've already seen, strong direction came from the districts. However, individual Aids were not powerless. Every Aid elected district delegates; delegates made up the District Board, and the Board voted on disbursement of all mission funds. "The following recommendations were adopted," reads one yearly district report, "Your delegates voted to carry them out" (10). Along with the Boxwork chair, it was the delegate's responsibility to educate the members of her Aid about mission causes. The records we studied show overwhelming support for whatever mission fields were assigned to them, in many cases going beyond recommendations, as seems to be hinted at in a note slipped inside the report from the national WMF convention in Minneapolis. "Here it is: that the Aids SHOULD NOT GIVE OUTSIDE THEIR OWN DISTRICTS unless asked to do…Let us give to our own in the Iowa District FIRST then after that we can branch out, if we have money and other gifts to spare" [emphasis at it appears in the original] (10).

By far the largest portion of benevolences went to WMF-sponsored causes through the district. Money went to foreign missions; money also went to more localized causes. From Bethlehem's Fort Dodge Circuit, mission box monies were "equally divided between Home and Foreign missions." A look at the titles of mission tracts and program materials dispersed to local Aids identifies some of WMF's home missions. "Our Mission Among Deaf and Blind" spoke to its connection to Ephpatha Missions at Faribault, Minnesota. Part of the WMF effort included translating mission materials into Braille and suitable printed material for the deaf. "Ministering to the Men of the Sea" informed members of the Seamen's Mission. Local Aids were encouraged to participate in letter-writing campaigns to all American servicemen and to take special seasonal collections for the military. "Christ for the Eskimo Too," "Christ for the Indians," and "The Personal Approach and the Negro American" attempted to address the needs of disadvantaged national groups and began to acknowledge America's tricky problems with racism. As seen in each of our churches, clothing, bedding, books, and school supplies were occasionally sent off to Alaska, to Indian reservations in the Dakotas, and to large inner cities like Chicago's. One enigmatic tract title—"Has God Forsaken the Jews?"—stands alone, as we found no direct donations to the Jewish community.

One very specific "home" gift of benevolence seems important to mention. Through several Depression years, Bethlehem's Ladies Aid met the pastor's salary when general congregational funds couldn't. From 1932-1936 records show the Aid contributed "half salary" and "one-month salary" at various times. There are also notations in two places indicating the Aid paid half of Trygve Lenning's "parochial school salary," amounting to $10.00, although it's not clear how many months that covered. As Bethlehem's *skolererer*, Lenning taught basic reading, writing, math, geography, and of course, Bible studies to the youth of the congregation. Yearly recorded mission totals varied from a low of $13.55 to a high of $48.50

during these five years. By 1937 the congregation was again able to meet salaries without contributions from the Aid, and mission donations increased steadily. It's hard to believe that Bethlehem would have been alone in this experience. It's *impossible* to believe that their mission totals wouldn't have been higher had they had the freedom to choose mission over salary.

"Not since the day of Pentecost has the urgency for evangelizing the world been felt more keenly than today," writes Grace Noll Crowell in the Fort Dodge Circuit Mission Report of 1948. "Even political and military leaders have openly said that the only hope lies in the power of the Christian message." Local Ladies Aid organizations were to understand that what they did had national import, even to Washington and the White House. Through its foreign mission program, the WMF provided women with a vision to change the world. Farmwives in Emmons and Lime Creek knew that the pennies they dropped into penny-a-meal boxes would buy food for families somewhere in Africa. Trinity women knew that canned goods from their home pantries would feed a dormitory of orphaned girls in Wisconsin. In Buffalo Center women were assured that the quilts they sewed and the clothes they collected would warm Indian children in Alaska. Mission work empowered. It gave the Ladies a political voice, and it made them strong. Through the Ladies Aids of the WMF, rural women built college libraries and Bible camps, put Bibles into the hands of Japanese children, sent mittens and scarves to America's servicemen, wrote letters to Columbian missionaries, and bought corn to feed the hungry all over the world. Their imaginations were fueled; they were connected; they went beyond themselves.

CHAPTER SEVEN
WE LOSE; WE GAIN

We dedicated the new church building the same year as the ALC
merger came through. It all came of a piece: new building, new
hymnals, and new women's organization. We had a social hall with
a real kitchen for LCW meetings and big doings, the library
and kitchenette for Circle.

—Ellen

"On the virtue of its women, so a nation rises or falls."

GOODBYE TO LADIES AID

And goodbye to Alma, Marita, and Linnea. It's time to leave the imaginary behind for the living. We listen once more.

In 1960 four Lutheran church bodies banded together to become the American Lutheran Church (ALC). The old American Lutheran Church (formerly the separate Iowa Synod and Joint Synod of Ohio, mostly of German tradition), the Evangelical Lutheran Church (also known as the Norwegian Lutheran Church of America), and the United Evangelical Lutheran Church (the Danish synod) combined under one umbrella. In 1963 they were joined by some congregations formerly belonging to the Lutheran Free Synod. Within the structure of the ALC was a new women's organization, ALCW. Emmons, Bethlehem, and Trinity women exchanged their affiliation with the Women's Missionary Federation for the new synod organization.

In 1988 the Evangelical Lutheran Church (ELCA) in America was formed by combining the ALC, the Association of Evangelical Lutheran Churches, and the Lutheran Church in America. The women's organization is now Women of the ELCA or WELCA.

Ann remembers the formation of ELCA as a time marked in Emmons by the challenge to learn the green hymnal's new liturgies. Otherwise, the transition to new identity went smoothly. Similarly, almost thirty years earlier, I remember Emmons' adoption of the ALC red hymnal, but I also recall real trauma among congregants. The beginnings of the ALC coordinated with a new building. Saying goodbye to our beloved old white clapboard was difficult, even though it was literally falling down around us, was being encroached upon by a building project at the school next door, and had long been too small.

The timing of a new building with a new synodical designation heightened what we were leaving behind. For the entire history of Emmons, the congregation had known itself as people of Norwegian heritage. There were other Europeans among us, but our predominance was Norwegian, and our church history had always been thus. We identified ourselves as separate from the Germans, the Danes, the Swedes, and the Finns. Ellen sums it up for us: "The things that bothered most were the differences between the Lutheran churches—the Swedish, the Finnish, the Norwegians—themselves, not between differing denominations. It took a long time for the German church and our Lutheran church to come together. And you can still hear it from some of the older ones."

The actual move was made on a sunny Sunday morning. Every woman, man, and child carried something—hymnals, altar furnishings, Bibles, choir robes—in a ceremonial procession across field and highway to our new digs where we held a celebratory service. I carried a candle. In the photographs, you see beaming faces; behind the scenes, along with the joy of new beginnings, there was the sadness of leaving much of the old and dear behind. It's helpful to mark such transitions with ceremony. Ceremony allows for the expression of all the different emotions that accompany change.

We can't help but note that our Ladies aren't getting much of a ceremony as the sort of service they've always provided is changing and being replaced by new ways.

Women of the ELCA is not a reincarnation of the Ladies Aid or even of ALCW. It's an organic, dynamic association designed to meet the needs of contemporary church women, *organic* in the sense that it arose from felt need—as did the Ladies Aid more than a century ago—and *dynamic* in that it will to continue to evolve as needs change. Their stated mission is to "mobilize women to act boldly on their faith in Jesus Christ" (http://www.womenoftheelca.org). This commitment is carried out in a global mission as they respond to the ravages of war, natural disasters, hunger, disease, poverty, ignorance, and whatever affects women's physical, mental, and spiritual well-being. Particularly committed to education, WELCA strives to disseminate fair and just information about economics, the environment, medicine, culture, even politics. They're not the Ladies Aid, but were it not for the Ladies' groundwork, they wouldn't exist. Furthermore, one would be hard pressed to find former Aid members who don't find satisfaction and gratification in the existence of WELCA. Bev from Trinity sums it up: "WELCA is the granddaughter of the Ladies Aid. Every Aid member should be proud of how she taught today's women to think globally."

"I THINK IT WILL BE FUN TO GET TOGETHER TO WORK"

Ann has her monthly quilting group. I have my monthly needlepoint meeting. The needlepoint group came together under somewhat unusual circumstances. The congregation I belong to now is fifty years old. Their membership is and always has been comprised mostly of professional people. We've never had a Ladies Aid. Neither has there ever been an association with ALCW or WELCA. The needlepoint group is more like a "club" that formed organically. A few years ago, during a building expansion project, my friend Margareta had a vision that the congregation should make kneelers for the altar railing in our new sanctuary. The Council approved the project; a designer was hired to create the design; yarn, canvas, and stretchers were purchased. And then we hit a roadblock: our new sanctuary design didn't include a traditional altar rail. No place for kneelers.

The materials were bagged and stored, some of the original group of needleworkers—including Margareta—moved away, and mostly the project was forgotten.

Twelve years later, Margareta returned, rejoined, and had the idea to resurrect. She found it sad that all those expensive materials had not been used. We didn't have to make kneelers, she pointed out; the design could be altered to create a mural above our sanctuary entrance. "I think it will be fun to get together to work," she said. She set about gathering workers again, sending out a general email invitation. The response was a delightful and surprising mix of ages, income levels, and life styles. Our group includes two former council presidents, a designer, a school teacher, two first generation American immigrants, a Jewish woman, a banker, a college professor, and a medical social worker. We're young and old and in between.

Tonight's meeting begins with Margareta leading prayer and inviting each woman to share a blessing since we last met. Those few moments unite us, and then the real conversation and the real work—which might be one and the same—of the evening commences. There's talk about one woman's impending engagement which is met with emotional support and advice and followed by a discussion about someone's abusive first marriage. That leads to talk about marriages based on friendship. As we stitch, the topic changes to an impending mission trip to an orphanage in Guatemala. Someone mentions the collection of fabrics brought back from a mission trip to Africa the year before and wonders if the woman traveling to Guatemala might look for native fabrics. There's comparison of individual needlepoint styles, and we talk about how the repetitive motion relaxes and centers our minds. We consider needlework's restorative powers. An evening's chatter rises and wanes, flits from topic to topic. We examine many problems but solve few. No matter. Our souls are fed as we stitch. We have come to understand that it's important for us to be together and work in concert.

Our kind of gathering is becoming rare. Today's women find it difficult to impossible to hold "Ladies Aid" in the ways of the past. My group is a purposeful anomaly, and we treasure it. We've loosely organized ourselves around a common project that will one day enhance our shared worship space. The idea of the project was conceived more than a decade ago, and it's taken us this long to bring it to fruition; such is the busy-ness of our lives. Families, jobs, professions, home duties, shopping, kids' soccer games, civic organizations... The list that claims us is long. But tonight, we come together purposefully because we understand the value of being women in community and of doing some of the same things as the Ladies. They taught us so much. Their work and their dialogue paved the way for us.

On another day, Ann and I attend an actual Ladies Aid meeting (WELCA) in Emmons. Ann is the featured speaker this afternoon, invited to tell the Ladies about her work with international college students. As we look over the group we recognize most of the faces. Emmons is our home church. Ann was baptized here. Both of us were confirmed and married in this church. Our mother Agnes, our Grandma Clara, and many of our aunts were leaders in the Aid. How many terms as president would they have shared among them? How many district conventions? How many lutefisk suppers? In the group today we recognize cousin Gloria, Aunt Lucille and Aunt Berdine, Muriel, Vonnie, Viola, Kerjil, and Ellen, all close friends of our mother, many of whom come over to tell us how much they still miss her. "She always spoke the truth," says one. "And you could always hear her voice stand out."

Mom's voice *did* stand out. She didn't sing well, but she always sang loudly. As children, that embarrassed us. She stood out in a lot of ways, for a while as a single mom in the 1950s after my father died, and always as a working mom, even after she married the man who would become Ann's father. Yet she always made time in her busy life for church, and that included Aid and her Dorcas Circle. In church her voice rang out strongly, especially at the blessing. "And also with YOU," she'd say as though she really meant it, as though she were addressing the pastor personally.

Aunt Berdine has invited Ann today. When we arrive, Berdine rushes to welcome us, taking each into her arms and with typical Norwegian self-effacement, apologizing for troubling us by complicating our schedule with her Aid meeting. Indeed, as the afternoon unfolds, we hear apologies from many of the Ladies. They feel bad there isn't a larger audience; they regret not being able to ask Ann more challenging questions; they apologize for their advanced ages and that there's no one from the younger generation to carry on their work when they're too old or gone. We notice that no one in the group is younger than 70.

The business meeting begins with a treasurer's report. Expenses to date include a magazine subscription for Pastor Julie, kitchen supplies, contributions toward the youth camping trip, dishwasher repair, and the organ fund. The Lutefisk Supper Committee gives an update. An announcement about a WELCA district gathering later in the month with a plea for attendees meets with groans, while there is some interest in having luncheon exchanges with area WELCA groups ($5.00 per lunch).

Then Ann takes the floor to talk about her role as a college ESL director (English as a Second Language). I think about how in the 1930s the Ladies Aid was consciously, purposefully leaving languages other than English behind them, moving beyond their immigrant status, and embracing Americanism. Today they're welcoming a new kind of immigrant diversity. When Ann asks how many have traveled overseas to a country where English is not dominant, a third of them raise their hands.

Ann and I enjoy sheetcake, coffee, nuts, and lemonade with the Ladies. At the end, we leave among many hugs and fond farewells. Before we go, they issue the biggest apology of all: Pastor Julie has forgotten to attend their meeting.

The Ladies' apologies echo sadly. We know they've seen—are seeing—the demise of something their female ancestors envisioned, something of which they've been a part that's bigger than themselves. The efforts of their mothers, aunts, and grandmothers prearranged for them the sort of organization that afforded much satisfaction. At the very least, it afforded friendship, fellowship, and mentorship. It gave both structure and identity to their lives. Even more, it was the channel through which they made donations to the local community and to the world beyond. It connected them to larger conversations. Perhaps most importantly, at least to their congregations, it gave a means for the parish to get the work done, both holy and mundane. At the onset of their womanhood, it had seemed so easy to enter into avenues laid out by those who went before. Now they are acutely aware that an easy entry structure has not been provided for the next generation. Though they wouldn't want to give up hard-won equities for their daughters and granddaughters, those equities have made life infinitely more complex for them, for the men in their lives, and for their congregations. Who will do the work? they ask.

On another day, we sit in on a circle meeting at Bethlehem. Besides Ann and me, eleven women are present. Pastor Perry leads a short Bible study from the first verses of Mark and shares some prayer concerns of the congregation. There are announcements about whose turn it is among the circles to serve coffee after Sunday worship and about the next needlework project. As to the needlework project, one of the women leans forward and confides to Pastor Perry, "If 'someone' volunteers, tell her I don't need her help, if you catch my drift." "Someone" turns out to be the same woman associated with the disappearance of the quilt some years ago. Before we leave, we have "lunch" (sheetcake, coffee, nuts, and lemonade).

MEETING THE CHALLENGE OF CHANGE

In the writing of this book, Hermoine, Gwen, and Esther have all died. Hermoine at 83 was the youngest and Esther at 98, the oldest. These women had become our friends, and we grieve. From their patience with our first tentative questions to their eventual impatience with the slowness of the project's progress ("The story really needs to be told!"), they were unfailingly generous and exuberant. Their passing underscores the need for immediacy.

Reality is that our time with the Ladies is growing shorter; we won't have any of them much longer. Even many of the buildings in which they toiled are disappearing, replaced by newer edifices that better meet modern church needs. In the process, much of their history is in jeopardy. One day a few years ago, I drove out to see Lime Creek Lutheran. This was Mom's childhood church, located three miles due west of Emmons, Minnesota, on the north side of State Line Road. An ubiquitous white clapboard building perched on a slight hill where its spire could be seen a mile in either direction, its grounds were circumferenced with graves. Wrought iron fenced the whole with an imposing front gate over which "Lime Creek Lutheran" curved in iron letters.

On this particular day, I nose my car up to the black fence and step out into clumps of weeds edging their way through the smattering of a leftover gravel parking area. There had never been a real parking lot, only the broad shoulder of a country road. State Line Road had been paved mid-century, but standing here outside the gate, it is still easy to envision buggies lining the fence, their horses pawing the dirt, snorting and nickering till services were over.

I come now because I know the old building is slated for removal. I want to see it one last time in its natural setting, surrounded by the cemetery where *Bestamor* Brita, *Bestafar* Ole, Grandma Clara, and Grandpa David lay buried.

The wind is blowing fiercely. It always blows here. The church and cemetery sit—sat—on a slight hill, surrounded by corn fields. Nothing breaks the wind. I remember as a small child sitting in the sanctuary at holiday services, listening as much to the roar of wind as to what was going on at the altar, feeling the walls shudder as the white clapboard exterior bore the brunt. Still, it stood strong, fast, solid, safe. Like a church should be. It felt like it would last forever.

On this day I thread my way through the cemetery, my shoulder bent into the howling wind. I pause only briefly to note tombstones of family members. If it weren't so windy, I'd explore the cemetery, but it's cold, and I need shelter. The back basement door is unlatched, and I let myself in to the stone-walled chamber. Down five steps to the basement floor, I push open another door to hear the scrabbling of tiny feet. I'm in the old fellowship hall. The electricity has been turned off, but no matter; afternoon sunlight floods through the row of casement windows. I finger what's left of the curtains and run my hands along the white-washed walls. Leaning against the walls are a few broken metal folding chairs; all the useable furniture has been removed. Beneath my feet is crumbling linoleum laid over a cement floor.

At the rear, behind a service counter (directly under the altar) is the kitchen. To my adult eyes, it looks surprisingly small to have produced hundreds of thousands of meals over the years. Many hands worked here. In the whole of the surrounding communities, there's probably not a single person whose mother, grandmother, or aunt didn't work in this kitchen at least once. Now the white enameled cupboards are mostly bare. I open each cabinet; there's a metal serving tray in one, a coffee urn in another. My grandma used these things. Too bad they're too big for my suitcase.

When I find a lone china creamer shoved into a corner, I pick it up, dust it off, and pocket it.

Next to the kitchen is the bathroom. The door hangs loose; its walls are constructed of flimsy wood paneling. Behind the bathroom, separated off by draperies—no walls—is a nursery. As I enter I see something disappear into the far wall: a mouse? rat? There's a crib with missing slats, a wooden rocking chair, and a faded Cradle Roll poster still hanging on the wall, ink so aged it's impossible to pick out the names.

Upstairs I find the sanctuary. Here furnishings are almost intact. I walk down the aisle and recognize the creaking floor. I run my hand from pew to pew, leaving hand tracks in the dust. Halfway the distance to the altar, I help myself to a hymnal from a pew rack (but not before I find a tissue to wipe away evidence of the critter I saw downstairs). Inside the front cover someone's written "In Memory of" with the name of my second cousin. I pocket the hymnal.

At the front is the altar. There's an elaborately carved communion rail, a kneeling step with worn red velvet, and an oil painting of Christ the Shepherd by a former local artist. The pulpit hangs off the front side wall. In mind's eye I see Pastor Hanson. He wears his black and white vestments and green Trinity stole. Wispy-pale hair and paper-thin features match his voice, so soft you'll miss it if you so much as breathe too hard. Mrs. Hanson (if I ever knew her given name, I've forgotten it!) sits in the front pew. She'll lead the singing, and after the service, she'll join her husband at the door as he greets parishioners. Her business will be finding out who's ill and needs meals delivered, arranging devotions at Circle, and reminding folks about Aid meeting.

Memories are thick. But I note something missing. Some*one* is missing. Opposite the pulpit is an empty space where the organ used to sit. Were it still there, Aunt Cora would be on the bench. After church, after her postlude, I'd run up to say hello and run my fingers over the keys. She'd tell me not to forget my organ lesson this week. And the two of us would have gone downstairs, arm in arm, to share after-service refreshments, prepared by women of the Circle whose turn it was to serve the event.

By now it's late afternoon, and the light is waning. I take my treasures and leave.

A year later, Ann and I return. The church is gone, and the basement hole has been filled in. Surrounded by tombstones, the footprint now leaves space to enlarge the cemetery. At the center is a small monument.

We drive to the living history museum where the church building has been relocated. Lime Creek Church was lifted and rolled onto flatbed moving platforms and driven ten miles down the road. One day Ellen showed us a sequence of photos her son had taken of the move: "Church on Rollers," "Church on Gravel Road," "Church Driven out of Sight." Lime Creek still stands, but it's a church without a congregation. Occasionally special services are held here now, for holidays mostly. In a sense it belongs to more rather than fewer, and that's good. I'm also glad it's part of a living testament, albeit a museum, rather than a restaurant like one of the old churches in my town. (Although, you *could* make the argument that food service would be a fitting testament...) There's no basement. Here occasional holiday worshippers will recall their childhood Christmas services, but they'll walk out the door knowing they're missing something—no lutefisk dinner with *lefse* and *krumkake* waits downstairs.

Change is not bad. This particular change has been made to allow for new growth, a very good thing. But change is difficult, sometimes painful, and always a time when we need to notice particularly carefully what is happening: what we gain, and what we lose. For Lime Creek, the transition from active congregation to museum took many painful conversations. To the members at Lime Creek, dissolving the congregation and disseminating membership to other area churches, creating a board of trustees to oversee the physical property, and making arrangements to relocate the building took many years. Real people were involved, people whose life-time of worship experience—experience built on lively memories of ancestral worship patterns—had to undergo radical change. Lime Creek's demise illustrates the experience of many rural congregations as a once vital way of life gives way to the new.

Lime Creek is particularly interesting to us because it's become symbolic to people in the area of the passing on of the old Lutheran Ladies Aid. Until 1960, Lime Creek was a two-point congregation, sharing a pastor with Emmons. Along with its sister church, it belonged to the Evangelical Lutheran Church. Over the years, Lime Creek's membership dwindled while the town congregation's grew. Commensurate with the formation of the ALC, the town church voted to call its own pastor. Lime Creek struggled to support a pastor on its own. The synodical merger created a new women's organization, and the familiar "Ladies Aid" was left behind. In actively growing congregations, changing from Aid to ALCW was positive; at Lime Creek, it was loss.

THE CHANGE IN WOMEN'S ROLES

On the Sunday after Ann's talk at WELCA, we listened to Pastor Julie preach. Pastor Julie and her husband are part of a new breed: pastoring couples. Between them they share three congregations. This was the first Sunday in Advent and her topic was "What do we want Jesus to find us doing when he returns?" Pastor Julie's message was that Jesus would want to see us letting people know how valuable they are. She baptized a little girl that morning, a child perhaps a year old. "She'll be a witness to everyone around her," said Pastor Julie. "She'll tell someone about the Gospel. In the same way, you tell people about the Gospel by your presence in the world. You are valuable. You are this baby girl; you are every person." The child was the daughter of an unmarried couple, a stark contrast to even a generation ago. Mom would have liked Pastor Julie.

During announcement time, Pastor Julie publicly admitted that she'd forgotten to attend WELCA earlier in the week. She was chagrined and apologetic, and she was easily forgiven, even as her absence seemed to underscore the Ladies' uncertainty about the future. Since the era of Ladies Aid, there's been a sea change in the way a woman's calling is viewed. Our Ladies often talked about "servanthood" and about how its original meaning has been lost. Servanthood was a high calling in earlier ages. "I'm glad I was able to serve," says Vi. "Servanthood was important to us. No matter how much I gave, to the Ladies, to the pastor, I was glad to give to them." The Ladies Aid served. Their job was to be to the congregation whatever it needed—janitors, chefs, organizers, spiritual guides, teachers, fundraisers. They maintained its daily activity. They served each other; they served the community and the world through their mission work; they served the pastor.

"The pastor was the leader," says Hermoine. "And the pastor's wife. She was someone who stood a bit above the regular Aid member." As she talked about the role that a pastor's wife served in the congregation, by turns spiritual leader, organizer, and proxy for her husband, we asked whether she remembered talk among the Ladies about feminism. Hermoine seemed surprised. "Feminism? We didn't think much about it. I think women thought they were doing so much in trying to raise the money and so on and so forth, there wasn't time for feminism." Feminism, she says, brings up a lot of "those 'self' words; you know, self-reliance, self-awareness. Those are pretty dangerously close to selfishness. We were more thinking about self*less*ness."

Hermoine continues, "When it came to the church organization itself, we didn't want the men to abdicate. I think we thought if a lot of the women started taking over, it would allow the men to say, Well, that's great, we don't need to worry about that any more! In time, we're seeing differently, that women and men can share the same responsibilities." Twelve years ago Hermoine's church, Trinity, called its first female pastor. The Ladies have been accepting and supportive.

As Vi tells, "I think the feeling at Trinity about women pastors was 'that's okay, but we're never going to want one.' You know? It took a while. But weren't we lucky to get Pastor Dannie Jo?" We ask about women bishops. "They make good ones! The work that a pastor has to do, that's the kind of work women have always done."

Trinity and Emmons have each hired a female pastor, and Bethlehem has already been served by two. In Emmons, where the main Ladies Aid (WELCA) monthly attendance has dropped from one hundred fifty to twenty, the number of circles has decreased to four, about half of what it once was. These four are assigned to serve funerals by turn, to serve and provide programs for WELCA meetings, and to provide general maintenance duties for the parish (Sunday morning nursery care, extra cleaning, coverage of Altar Guild duties, etc.). This parallels Trinity and Bethlehem.

All of this was illustrated when Ann and I attended Aunt Cora's funeral last year. This was the same Aunt Cora who played the organ at Lime Creek and from whom I took lessons. She'd also been a Sunday school teacher, Aid officer, and a lifelong faithful servant of the church. In rural communities such as this, boundaries are blurred and church continues out into the community. Aunt Cora would have interpreted whatever she did in the community as an extension of faith, so for her, church work included being 4-H leader and holding civic office. It included family life, in which she was mother, foster mother, adoptive mother, and wife of our politically-minded, community activist uncle.

Aunt Berdine—now a spritely 89 years old—was the liveliest and the most agile of the Ladies in the kitchen at the funeral. Her co-hostesses were limited physically, one using a walker, one a cane. They stayed in the kitchen, propped up against the counter, cutting and serving sheetcakes, filling juice glasses, and washing dishes. Aunt Berdine circled fellowship hall with a coffee pot and trays of extra desserts. After the funeral, in family discussion about how Aunt Berdine wasn't afforded the luxury of visiting with fellow mourners (or how Aunt Berdine wouldn't allow herself the privilege?), Ann's husband Perry—a pastor dealing with the challenge of servanthood in his own congregation—surmised that in the very near future, all such events would necessarily be catered.

It isn't that younger women don't care about or participate in the work of the church. It's that today they experience very different demands on their time. Many have professional careers beyond the home. The demands of home life itself are greater. The average family might have fewer children today, but lifestyles have made each child more labor intensive, illustrated by the number of extra-curricular activities each one is expected to pursue. Standards of housekeeping, cuisine, and personal upkeep have all increased from our mothers' and grandmothers' expectations. Modern "labor-saving machines" actually *add* work hours because each one heightens social expectations.

Perhaps most importantly, today's women are of a different philosophy. They tend to value their time in terms of what it's worth monetarily, and they recognize that servanthood doesn't necessarily have to be gendered. And therein lies new territory. Pastors are both men and women; women of the church no longer look exclusively to male leadership; men of the church no longer expect that women do all the menial jobs.

In Ann and Perry's church where they'll "just have to cater everything," the solution presents a complicated set of ethics. On the one hand, paying for services which used to be provided *gratis* affirms the work of the Ladies. On the other, the fact that the women themselves were never paid, and the sure knowledge that if the old system were to continue they *still* wouldn't be paid, makes them uncomfortable. "What a typically masculine solution to a problem," one told us. "Throw money at it." Judging Aunt

Berdine's activity and enthusiasm, she's not eager to give up her responsibilities. She finds identity and worth as a Christian through her servanthood. Take that away, and she diminishes. We Lutherans have always believed strongly in a sense of vocation or calling, the assigning by God of jobs and responsibilities, each proper and valuable. While that's good theology, it has also been turned on its head as an excuse to think about some kinds of useful activity as repression rather than as servanthood, especially in discussions over gender.

We interviewed pastors and church members concerned about the future of all socially-based groups, especially church groups, and not only the Ladies Aid. Many predict that such groups won't be sustainable unless they have specific purposes for organizing and specific end dates. Twenty-first century people know that few have the time or desire to attend meetings for the sake of attending meetings. Our lives are too busy; we demand purpose. I think of my needlepoint group and the satisfaction we're all feeling from the chance to work and talk together around a central project; we have a *purpose*, and we also have an *end date*.

New definitions of servanthood will also come from increased gender awareness. Already in Emmons, Bethlehem, and Trinity there's a more equitable sharing of responsibility which parallels trends in the general population. These congregations have come a long way from the days when women had no voice save through their husbands. They recognize women have as much to offer as men, and that male congregants won't necessarily abdicate all responsibility when women take leadership positions.

In my young congregation, only a third as old as Emmons, Bethlehem, and Trinity, the daily life of the congregation was planned and carried out from the beginning by committees or teams equally populated by men and women. As I said earlier, it never had a Ladies Aid or an organized women's group, and we have always found alternate ways of getting the work done. If women's Ladies Aids as they were in the first half of the twentieth century are gone, that's not altogether good, but it's not completely bad, either. The Ladies' challenge to us is to discover ways of serving and worshipping that suit twentieth-first century life styles. To quote both Hermoine and Ellen, "We move on."

As we move on, we recognize, give credit, and honor those who paved our way. The Ladies quite literally built the Lutheran church we know today. They were practical and resourceful women who got the job done, and in the process, they had little patience for self-importance, haughtiness, presumption, or self-aggrandizement. They functioned from a servant approach that always translated itself into action. What mattered most to them was caring for each other.

A FULL CIRCLE OF STORIES

As we write this final chapter, we enter yet another Christmas season. On the one hand, we're tempted to think we should have devoted an entire chapter to the holidays; after all, these are the times when we Norwegian Americans are most "Norwegian." I am gratified to know that at this very moment, plans are underway for a traditional Christmas Eve service at Lime Creek, the very same sanctuary where I sat with anticipation listening to the wind so many Christmases ago, albeit at a new location. With a little luck whoever is planning this year's celebration will be able to find someone who can preach in the Norwegian language—or recite a prayer. At the very least, the congregation will be invited to sing "*Jeg Er Saa Glad I Julekveld*" ("I Am So Glad Each Christmas Eve"), the hymn we all learned as children.

On the other hand, our Norwegian-ness at Christmas is a sort of secondhand identity, meaning that it's perhaps not as genuine as we'd like to believe, but one that "out-Norwegians the Norwegians." I talked about this idea with my Swedish friend Margareta. She came to the States thirty years ago to begin a Scandinavian import business in Maine, but between business trips back and forth and close family ties, she knows the Sweden of today isn't the Sweden of her childhood. Customs change; politics change; living standards change; fashion changes. Over the years she has connected with many first-generation immigrants from her home country and observes that "Yes, we out-Swede the Swedes! We like to think that whatever we remember from our time in that country is the way it is today." In her import shop, at Christmastime customers wanted traditional straw ornaments and painted wooden horses, things not necessarily found in modern Swedish households.

Besides, Lutherans aren't nearly so homogenous now as we were between 1930 and 1959, and that's a good change. Look out over the faces in our congregations today and it's evident that things are changing. In my own New England church there are Japanese, Indonesian, Guatemalan, African, Mexican, and Korean faces among the European. Some of our members speak English as their second language. In Emmons, Bethlehem, and Trinity too there are new faces. We are so much more culturally rich. It's now important that lessons learned from our American brand of Norwegian-ness are tempered by a new, broader identity.

There's a second reason why we've chosen to forgo a separate holiday chapter. While the Ladies always had a major role to play at Christmas, in many ways it was simply a ramping up of the sorts of activities they carried out all year round. There were Sunday school drama rehearsals to direct, costumes to be sewn for the cast—how many shepherds and angels this year?—and the final production presented, all of which would have been handled by the Ladies (more than likely under the direction of a male Sunday school principal). The decorating of the sanctuary and fellowship hall would have fallen to them. They would have coordinated any sort of special projects—gifts to the pastor, special gifts for individuals or causes they supported, special holiday meals, etc. But while time-consuming and even arduous, these were natural extensions of business as usual.

My earliest Lutheran Christmas memories are of being an angel in the pageant, perhaps the same for most of today's youngest children—no matter which current drama the director orders, the littlest ones get relegated to angels or animals! They don't mind. In fact, it's always exciting. "I'm going to be a fairy again this year!" my five-year-old granddaughter Merete announces. She means angel, not fairy, but in what seems to be a national obsession with fairy princesses by all five-year-olds, the wearing of wings and halo is magical, and fairies equal angels in the miraculous. "Grandma, remember when you told me about the angels singing in the sky?"

Finally, as another year comes to a close, Ann and I come full circle from where we began. We have lived inside the Ladies' stories, and we are grateful for that privilege. Their stories teach. They give us a sense of being alive. They make meaning. They make it possible for us to touch the holy.

The Ladies have done well. All of them, Esther, Vi, Ellen, Hermoine, Gwen, Bev, Berdine, Cora, and the rest. Our journey with them has been all gain. Getting to know them has changed us in profound ways. Because of them, Ann and I know a little more about who we are. And when I forget, when I need reminding, I have a creamer and a hymnal.

When I think about it, of two randomly pocketed artifacts, neither could be more appropriate as symbols of all the Ladies did, who they were, and what they leave us. One captures the essence of the kind of service they embodied—enriching the experience of fellowship at every turn whatever the need, whatever the occasion—while the other speaks of and to worship—the peculiarly Lutheran style in which song and liturgy urge us toward holiness.

As we've explored in the last chapters, the Ladies were the bridge between very different eras, and they've led the church gracefully from one to the other. We talked in chapter one of the industrial changes effected in their lifetimes, and throughout we've assumed something about the social transformations that accompanied them. Our Ladies have also been at the center of how society has changed its notions over what it means to be a woman, specifically a woman of faith. Incorporated into one of the old histories in one of The Boxes was the declaration that "On the virtue of its women, so a nation rises or falls," giving a backward nod to the Victorian "cult of domesticity." An ideal Victorian woman exhibited in her personality four central virtues (piety, purity, submissiveness, and domesticity), thereby making it possible for the men of a nation to attain greatness. While the Ladies operated partially within the leftover constraints of such by-gone thinking—pre-suffrage and pre-equality—they also drove us steadily forward by challenging the next generation to move beyond to a time when "virtue" could be shouldered more equally. Their dignity and ingenuity showed the way. They saw both limitations and possibilities, collectively if not individually. And so it was so often the ethos of the group that drove things forward, even while individuals embraced the status quo.

The ethos of the Ladies Aid: service and worship that always looked to the future. Serviceful worship and worshipful service. As they hand off to us their understanding of what makes a life of faith, how will we interpret their ethos for our lives? Lutheran women today are who we are because the Ladies hand us the freedom to internalize service and worship. They've made it possible for women to encompass multiple identities, from cooks and custodians, servants and supporters to pastors and church leaders. The Ladies give us choice.

What will we give our daughters and granddaughters? "Grandma," asks Merete as we're driving one day in the car. "Where does God live?" Assuming that she's asking about heaven, I embark on a theological discussion of unseen worlds, of the differences between reality and spirit, and of the God-ness within each of us. She's quiet for a while. I glance at her in the rearview mirror and see her scowling.

"Merete, do you have another question?" I ask.

"No. Not now."

"Then why the serious face?"

"I just wanted to know if he lives in the church always or just sometimes, and when he does, who takes care of him."

So we had a nice chat about God being everywhere all the time (not as difficult for a five-year-old to comprehend as for an adult who knows something about physical science) and about how each of us has her own responsibilities in "taking care of God" (also easy when you're five, and the adults who love and care for you are pretty much equal to God).

Merete's question has merit for our entire project. The Ladies were all about taking care of God. Who, indeed, takes care of God today?

The answer, of course, is that we all must.

BIBLIOGRAPHY

DeBerg, Betty A., with Elizabeth Sherman. *Women and Women's Issues in North American Lutheranism: A Bibliography.* Augsburg Fortress; Minneapolis; 1992.

Friend, Rev. Dr. Howard E, Jr. *Recovering the Sacred Center.* The Pilgrim Press; Cleveland, OH; 2000. Included as forward to *With Sacred Threads: Quilting and the Spiritual Life* by Susan Towner-Larsen and Barbara Brewer Davis.

Gelbach, Deborah L.. *From This Land: A History of Minnesota's Empires, Enterprises, and Entrepreneurs.* Windsor Publications, Inc.; USA; 1988.

Gjerde, Jon, and Carlton C. Qualey. *Norwegians in Minnesota: The People of Minnesota.* Norwegian Historical Society Press in coordination with The Norwegian American Historical Association; St. Paul; 2002.

Jochens, Jenny. *Women in Old Norse Society.* Cornell University Press; Ithaca and London; 1995.

Lagerquist, L. Diane. *In America the Men Milk the Cows: Factors of Gender, Ethnicity, and Religion in the Americanization of Norwegian-American Women.* Carlson Publishing, Inc.; Brooklyn, NY; 1991. Chicago Studies in the History of American Religion series; Jerald C. Brauer and Martin E. Marty, editors.

Lagerquist, L. Diane. *The Lutherans.* Praeger; Westport, Connecticut; 1999.

Larsen, Erling. *Minnesota Trails: A Sentimental History.* T. S. Denison & Co.; Minneapolis; 1958. Issued in observance of the Minnesota State Centennial.

Lovoll, Odd S. *Norwegians on the Prairie: Ethnicity and the Development of the Country Town.* Minnesota Historical Society Press in cooperation with The Norwegian American Historical Association; St. Paul; 2006.

Martin, Janet Letnes and Allen Todnem. *Lutheran Church Basement Women: Lutefisk, Lefse, Lunch and Jell-O.* Redbird Productions; Hastings, Minnesota; 1992.

Meier, Peg. *Bring Warm Clothes: Letters and Photos from Minnesota's Past.* Minneapolis Star and Tribune; Minneapolis, Minnesota; 1981.

Meyer, Ruth Fritz. *Women on a Mission: Including a History of the Lutheran Women's Missionary League.* Concordia; St. Louis, Missouri; 1967.

Nichol, Todd W., editor. *Crossings: Norwegian-American Lutheranism as a Transatlantic Tradition.* Norwegian American Historical Association; Northfield, Minnesota; 2003.

Reishus, Martha. *Hearts and Hands Uplifted: A History of the women's Missionary Federation of the Evangelical Lutheran Church.* Augsburg Publishing Co.; Minneapolis; 1958.

Semmingsen, Ingrid. *Norway to America: A History of the Migration.* University of Minnesota Press; Minneapolis; 1978. Translated by Einar Haugen.

The Forty-Niner: The Villages of Alden and Conger and the Townships of Alden, Carlston, Mansfield and Pickerel Lake. Alden, Minnesota; 1949.

Towner-Larsen, Susan and Barbara Brewer Davis. *With Sacred Threads: Quilting and the Spiritual Life.* The Pilgrim Press; Cleveland, Ohio; 2000.

Vanberg, Bent. *Of Norwegian Ways.* Harper and Row, Publishers; New York; 1970.

Warnke, Mabel. *China As I Saw It.* Vantage Press, Inc.; New York; 1984.

Willey, H. *50 Years of Life around Emmons.* Emmons Leader Publishing; Emmons, Minnesota; 1949.

Zempel, Solveig. *In Their Own Words: Letters from Norwegian Immigrants.* University of Minnesota Press in cooperation with The Norwegian American Historical Association; Minneapolis; 1991.

Archives of the Evangelical Lutheran Church in America; Chicago. www.elca.org/archives/missionaries/elcamissionaries.html)

Janssen Resource Center. Evangelical Lutheran Church in America, New England Synod; Worcester, MA. www.nesynod.org/resources.

Libraries of the Luther Seminary in St. Paul, Minnesota.

Lutheran Resource Center. Clear Lake, Iowa. www.lutheranresource-center.org

Norwegian American Historical Association; St. Olaf College, Northfield, Minnesota. www.naha@stolaf.edu/

U.S. Bureau of Labor Statistics www.bls.gov/ U.S. Bureau of Labor Statistics, consumer Expenditure Survey. www.census.gov/prod/www/statistical-abstract-us.html.

Women's Missionary Federation Convention Reports, Evangelical Lutheran Church, South Central District. Fort Dodge, Iowa. Report booklets from 1935-1957.

The "Boxes"

Bethlehem Lutheran Church library and archives. 201 4th St. NE, Buffalo Center, Iowa 50424.

Emmons Lutheran Church library and archives. 490 Pearl St., Emmons, Minnesota 56029.

Trinity Lutheran Church library and archives. Rural Route, Bricelyn, Minnesota 56014.

Index

A

B

DR. DOT RADIUS KASIK is an academic writing consultant and the author of numerous journal and magazine articles. She has served on the writing faculties of Salem State College in Massachusetts, the University of New Hampshire in Durham, and, most recently, Tumaini Lutheran University in Tanzania. Her academic work in gender studies informs her writing. She is a life-long Lutheran and lives on the New Hampshire seacoast with her husband.

ANN AALGAARD is a parent education coordinator for northern Iowa Empowerment. She served on faculty at Waldorf College in Iowa as Director of ESL. She and her family worship at Bethlehem Lutheran in Buffalo Center, Iowa.

LaVergne, TN USA
05 January 2010
168949LV00005B/6/P